"In this lively, well-written book, Britt Frank a_____
movement toward listening to rather than av_____
making you stuck. To use one of her great metaphors, what if anxiety is___
annoying feeling to ignore or medicate and instead is a warning light on your
mind's dashboard, indicating that something inside you needs attention? Frank's
has been quite a journey and I'm so glad she's courageous enough to share it, and
the wisdom it brought her, with us."

—Richard C. Schwartz, PhD, creator of the evidence-based Internal Family Systems
(IFS) therapeutic model and faculty member at Harvard Medical School

"In *The Science of Stuck* Britt Frank provides insights that enable individuals to
move from the rigidity and predictiveness of being stuck to flexibility, curiosity,
and social accessibility. Through relatable examples, we can develop skills to
feel safe enough to venture into relationships and novel experiences and learn
that being stuck is not a lifelong destiny."

—Dr. Stephen W. Porges, PhD, originator of the Polyvagal Theory,
professor of psychiatry at the University of North Carolina,
and a cofounder of the Polyvagal Institute

"This book is relevant for our modern, complicated lives and necessary for when
we need to get our lives back on track. This book will give you the information
you need to spark your curiosity with enough room to engage the necessary in-
ward journey of self-reflection. You might just replace that stack of self-help
books on your bedside table with this one essential guide."

—Arielle Schwartz, PhD, author of *The Complex PTSD Workbook*

"With down-to-earth language, enlivening inner-exercises, vivid humanness and
humor, Britt Frank invites you to explore the gap between your own inertia and
momentum. *The Science of Stuck* provides the precise compass you need to navigate
your way to freedom." —Nancy Levin, author of *Setting Boundaries Will Set You Free*

"*The Science of Stuck* will give readers a new perspective, a deep understanding
of anxiety, and a way out of anxiety. A book that is much needed in our post-
pandemic world." —Milagros Phillips, author of *Cracking the Healer's Code*

"Britt Frank gives us an exceptionally wholehearted explanation for why it's so
important to reframe anxiety. With researched clarity, she invites us to recon-
sider the 'anxiety disorder' paradigm and invite anxiety to the table. Britt's kind
direction asks us to pull up a chair beside our fears and become friends."

—Kelly McDaniel, LPC, NCC, author of *Ready to Heal* and *Mother Hunger*

"If you feel stuck in your life, you can't afford not to read this book. In her powerfully engaging and relatable style, Britt takes you on a practical journey through understanding the practical neuroscience of stuck and what it's going to take for you to get your life moving on your own terms. Highly recommended."

—Alex Howard, founder and chairman of The Optimum Health Clinic, creator of Therapeutic Coaching, and author of *Decode Your Fatigue*

"Britt has done a tremendous job pulling together a book which forces one to reflect on their life, relationships, weaknesses, and strengths. She drives home the points that we all have the opportunity to take control, we all have the right to succeed, and that it is ok to not be perfect, but bottom line—we must take accountability for our results. Reading this book will make you uncomfortable, but it will give you the tools and the confidence to get unstuck."

—Dennis Huber, President of MJH Consulting and former Executive Vice President at CenturyLink

"Britt Frank expertly, concisely, and humorously clarifies what 'stuck' really is, and how we can all wrench ourselves free—to step into who we are meant to be."

—Meredith Atwood, author of *The Year of No Nonsense*

"Staying stuck is one of the greatest obstacles to growth. Britt Frank explodes through the barriers of confusion and resistance to help us use the power of anxiety to get unstuck. Once we do, we'll see more clearly, think with an open mind, feel more positively, and act with clarity and conviction."

—Bob Rosen, PhD, founder of The Healthy Leader and author of eight books on leadership

"There is nothing wrong with us. That's just one of the many takeaways I have from *The Science of Stuck*. As someone who's struggled with an anxiety disorder most of my life, Britt's relatable writing coupled with science is exactly what all of us need when we're feeling stuck, lost, and even broken."

—Andrea Owen, author of *Make Some Noise* and host of the Make Some Noise podcast

"Using research, theory, and her own experience as a therapist, Britt Frank compassionately reminds us that our painful experiences have roots and meaning, and that even when we feel broken, there is always a way through. As a therapist I appreciated her research and examples of resilience, and as a human being I felt soothed by her reminders that I could trust and honor all parts of myself."

—Cathy Cassani Adams, author of *Zen Parenting* and host of Zen Parenting Radio

"*The Science of Stuck* is a must-read for anyone looking to identify and overcome the barriers that keep them from moving forward in life, feeling happy and fulfilled, and enjoying meaningful relationships."

—Dr. Jennifer Sweeton, PsyD, forensic psychologist and author of *The Trauma Treatment Toolbox*

The Science of Stuck

The Science
of *Stuck*

Breaking Through Inertia to Find Your Path Forward

Britt Frank, LSCSW

a TarcherPerigee book

tarcherperigee

an imprint of Penguin Random House LLC
penguinrandomhouse.com

Copyright © 2022 by Britt Frank
First trade paperback edition 2023
Penguin Random House supports copyright. Copyright fuels creativity, encourages diverse voices,
promotes free speech, and creates a vibrant culture. Thank you for buying an authorized edition
of this book and for complying with copyright laws by not reproducing, scanning, or distributing
any part of it in any form without permission. You are supporting writers and allowing
Penguin Random House to continue to publish books for every reader.

TarcherPerigee with tp colophon is a registered trademark of Penguin Random House LLC.

Most TarcherPerigee books are available at special quantity discounts for bulk purchase for sales
promotions, premiums, fundraising, and educational needs. Special books or book excerpts also can
be created to fit specific needs. For details, write: SpecialMarkets@penguinrandomhouse.com.

Library of Congress Cataloging-in-Publication data has been requested.

Hardcover ISBN: 9780593419441
eBook ISBN: 9780593419458
Trade paperback ISBN: 9780593542859

Printed in the United States of America
2nd Printing

Book design by Laura K. Corless

For little b.

CONTENTS

This book is a guide containing evidence-based and anecdotal practices, academic research, professional stories, and personal experiences. I see the world through the lens of a privileged white cisgender woman living in a Western culture. There are as many reasons for getting stuck as there are humans. The information in this book refers to those for whom choice, relative safety, and access to resources is readily available. The information in this book does *not* apply to situations of abuse, oppression, enslavement, severe and persistent mental illness, power differentials, or systemic racism. Any practices that encourage you to examine your self-talk or to "change your mind to change your mood" have the potential to be toxic and victim-blaming. As a general rule, "managing your thoughts" works *only* if you are in a safe environment where choices are available.

This information is not intended to be therapy or a replacement for mental health treatment. The tools and exercises do *not* have universal application to every person in every culture in every situation. The chapter on family dynamics assumes that your parents/caregivers have the capacity to manage themselves and refers specifically to modern Western cultural norms. There are cultural traditions, socioeconomic circumstances, and many other reasons why children may sometimes need to take on adult roles.

This book does not focus on or apply to situations of "stuckness" related to gender, sexuality, or social inequality.

Take what is useful and leave the rest. While psychological factors can often create physical symptoms, *always* go to a medical professional to rule out medical causes before you do anything else. Do not stop taking your medication without the supervision of a qualified medical professional. If you are currently addicted to a chemical, seek medical attention. It can be dangerous and even life-threatening to try to detox off certain drugs and alcohol without medical supervision. This information refers to changing patterns of *behaviors*, not to tapering off of substances. If you or someone you know is a danger to themselves or to others, put this book down and immediately go to the emergency room. Client identifying details have been changed.

The Science of Stuck includes information about mental illness, abuse, intimate partner violence, sexual trauma, grief, drug addiction, eating disorders, and other content that some readers may find triggering. If you need immediate support, call the National Suicide Prevention Lifeline at 1-800-273-8255.

Making friends in adulthood is a weird and awkward (read: barf emoji) phenomenon that nobody appropriately prepares you for. Who, pray tell, wants to vulnerably ask another adult, explicitly or not, "Would you like to be my friend?" The answer is nobody. It feels as gawky as being the new kid in school.

Well, a few years ago, I stumbled across a podcast interview of Britt on Meredith Atwood's show, *The Same 24 Hours*, that made me laugh out loud, nod every other minute, and even shout out an "Amen!" or two. Who is this hilarious, thoughtful, shame-slaying, truth-telling psychotherapist? "I wanna be *her* friend!"

If only I'd had this gem of a book to give me some solace (see chapter 6), but alas I did not and sent a dorky fan-girl DM to @brittfrank on Instagram.

Lucky for me, Britt has the ability to neutralize the discomfort of a clumsy social media "middle school cafeteria" moment in less than three seconds flat, because she's one of those rare people who truly delight in the wackiness of what the great psychologist Albert Ellis called "f*cked up, fallible humans."

Fast-forward two years, and Britt is not only my esteemed colleague, but also, more important, my dear friend.

Human behavior, you might have noticed, is a real son of a mother. We all struggle at one time or other with that maddening problem of *knowing* what to do and yet continuing not to do it. This is the great paradox of the human condition and, as such, is nothing new.

Saul of Tarsus, then known as Paul, wrote two thousand years ago in his letter to the Romans: "I do not understand my own actions. For I do not do what I want, but I do the very thing I hate." He then finishes the sentiment with this relatable statement: "For I have the desire to do what is right, but not the ability to carry it out." I think Saint Paul roundly hits the nail right on the head.

This internal internecine war, I believe, is the defining feature of stuckness. But, like the experience of happiness, the state of stuck is easier to define in metaphor (yes, Britt will teach you it's okay for behavioral scientists to venture into the language arts and use metaphor to great effect). Developmental psychologist and Harvard professor Robert Kegan, PhD, describes *stuck* as trying to drive a car with your feet on both the gas and the brakes. You have one foot pressed down on the gas (your good intentions) and the other foot slammed down on the brake (acting in opposition to those good intentions).

We're revving our engines while getting nowhere. It's exhausting.

Judging by the very fact you're holding this book in your hand, I imagine you're well acquainted with the merry-go-round of your mystifying behavior. And—I'm going to go out on a limb here—I might also surmise you're ready to get off that merry-go-round and maybe even leave the amusement park entirely.

Let me assure you that you've found the right guide to direct you toward the exit.

With her candor, humanity, and humor, Britt Frank will help you understand from a trauma-informed perspective why you're stuck (hint: it's not what you think!), what predictable events will knock you right back into stuck (pro tip: take this book home for the holidays), and how you can oil the stuck joints of your life and begin unsticking (note: there are actionable exercises in each chapter).

However, since you're evidently brave enough to admit there's an area of your life in which you find yourself circling the drain, I'm going to respect your courage and tell you the truth about this book. So here goes. It makes no promise of easy transformations. It pulls no punches. And it will undoubtedly pull down the kabuki screen of your life to reveal some stagnant gunk. Sound fun? No, probably not. But neither is being stuck!

If you are, as they say, truly sick and tired of being sick and tired, then stick with Britt. She's not offering you a sweet swill of snake oil; she's offering you effective and lifesaving psychological medicine. Her medicine, I might add, is well researched and engineered over years in the life lab of her own thriving therapy practice. A big bonus in this insta-expert world we live in.

Developmental growth through every stage from cradle to grave (yes, there are developmental stages even for us grown-ups) is fundamentally about the continual yet evolving tension between our drive to self-protect and our drive to self-transform. This tension between defense and enhancement, limit and possibility, is in essence the very act of hope itself. If we're all defense and limit and stuckness, there is no hope. Yet if we're all enhancement, possibility, and limitless growth, no hope is required.

Not only does this book offer hope to those of us who have become stuck, but it also teaches us that as we engage in this tension between our protection and our evolution, we in fact become a living act of hope.

Turn to the next page and commit to follow Britt Frank's wise and compassionate guidance, because you, dear reader, no matter how deeply embedded you are in your own manure, are hope itself. After all, that manure makes excellent fertilizer.

—Sasha Heinz, PhD, MAPP,
Developmental Psychologist and Coach

The Science
of *Stuck*

If the human brain were so simple that we could understand it, we would be so simple that we couldn't.

—Emerson M. Pugh

t's the end of a weekday. Your work is done. Your kids, if you have any, are in bed. Your obligations are all fulfilled. You've been meaning to start working out in the evenings, and you finally have a free night. You feel like you *should* go for a run—but what you *actually* do is sit on the couch* binge-watching your favorite series.

Or maybe you've been craving fulfillment in the form of a new job. You've learned all you can at your current position and it's time to move on. Life has finally settled down, and you feel like you *should* start applying for new jobs—but what you *actually* do is keep reporting to the job you've out-grown, no longer feeling rewarded or a sense of energy and purpose from it.

Maybe you're stuck in a toxic relationship. Stuck in food or body image issues. Stuck in the "I should" spiral of self-judgment. Stuck in family pressure. Stuck in shutdown mode, unable to make the leap between what you *know* to do and what you *actually* do. And the cherry on top of the shame sundae? You likely assume the problem is *you*.

You're *not* lazy. You're *not* crazy.† You're not weak, dumb, broken, defec-

---

* If you haven't already, watch *SNL*'s "Pro-Chiller Leggings" skit. You'll feel oh-so-seen.

† The word "crazy" is biologically inaccurate. There is no such thing as a "crazy" person. Having a mental illness or experiencing mental health symptoms does not make someone crazy. You'll

tive, or lacking in willpower. And despite what your nagging inner critic tells you, you *don't* have a motivation problem. There's something *else* behind your discarded self-care plans, abandoned to-do lists, and neglected goals. And the way forward is simpler than you'd think.

Why Should You Believe Me?

Despite a life that looks squeaky clean on paper (with a mahogany framed degree from a fancy school on the wall), I was queen of the hot mess express. On Wikipedia under *stuck*, you might find an old picture of me, Marlboro Menthol smoke billowing out of my mouth, stubbornly ignoring the mold (and mice) in my downtown L.A. apartment, reeling from yet another *disastrous* relationship, panic attack, or depressive episode.

I *know* what it's like to be stuck.

After graduating from Duke University, I abandoned intellectual pursuits and used my considerable manipulation skills to waste away at an advertising job that I loathed. My life was more *Smoke, Cry, Binge* than *Eat, Pray, Love*. When I could no longer numb out with anorexia, Vicodin, sugar, *Us Weekly*, love addiction, or denial, I joined a fundamentalist cult. Yes, a cult.

The bizarre religious practices effectively distracted me from painful feelings—kind of like a chew toy for my brain. Obeying nonnegotiable rules and following strict, regimented disciplines created the illusion of family and belonging. My highly sensitive, highly volatile system felt temporarily comforted by someone *else* telling me what to do and how to think. When cult life didn't pan out, I tried psychics, exorcisms, meditation, yoga, intermittent fasting, medication, being a good girl, being a bad girl, being real, being fake, and everything in between.

---

see the word "crazy" used in this book as a metaphor for how it feels when there's no apparent explanation for intense feelings/symptoms.

Nevertheless, stuck persisted.

The first time I caught a glimmer of possibility that things could change was during a support group. One evening a compassionate counselor put a hand on my shoulder and whispered in my ear as I lay bawling on the floor, snot pouring out of my nose, "Britt, you are *not* crazy." This simple statement unlocked a path that led me on a decade-long journey to discover why we do the things we do.

The bottom line? There is a *reason* that you're stuck—and it's *not* laziness.

Mental health is *not* a mental process—mental health is a *physical* process. For many of us, even our scariest symptoms are *not* mental illnesses—they're *body responses*. The trajectory of my entire life changed when I learned about body responses. Symptoms of borderline personality disorder, bipolar 2, clinical depression, and eating disorders all but vanished. Long-standing patterns of stuck were gone—and remain ancient history. Eventually I returned to graduate school and became a licensed psychotherapist. This book won't magically fix your finances, change your body, or cure disease, but it *will* show you how I got unstuck—and how you can too.

Why Read This Book?

You likely have a stack of books sitting on your nightstand. Wading through oceans of research can add more overwhelm to your already overwhelmed system. I've pulled together information from my own stack of books so you can have everything in one place—kind of like a CliffsNotes guide to self-help. We'll take a speedboat tour around relationships, habits, motivation, procrastination, and overwhelm. While it can be fun to drop anchor and plunge into the abyss, this book is intended to give you *just enough* information to get moving.

Each chapter also provides tasks you can complete in five minutes. One important caveat: All of the tools and techniques assume you have enough to eat, a safe enough place to live, and relative access to resources. There are as many reasons to get stuck as there are humans—and sometimes people are stuck because they have no choices. The causes of and solutions to severe and persistent mental illness, systemic racism, social inequality, patriarchal oppression, generational poverty, and extreme trauma go beyond the scope of this book.

How to Use This Book

Remember the Choose Your Own Adventure series? Rather than starting with the first page and ending with the last page, *you* decided how the story unfolded. Each time you sat down to read, you'd experience the material in a new way. Reading from start to finish has never worked for me, so I structured this book to be consumed in any order you want. You can choose one of three paths—each one provides a different strategy to work through the information.

Path 1. *"I have no time."*

You don't have to read the whole book. Pick whatever topics catch your eye and jump straight to the end of each chapter. You'll find a bullet list summary, a brief section on dos and don'ts, and five-minute challenges that can be implemented *today*. You'll notice footnotes as you move through the material—feel free to skip over them.

Path 2. *"I'm curious to know more, but I don't have a lot of time."*

Read any chapters that feel applicable. If your family is awesome but you can't stop procrastinating, skip the family section and head to chapter 3, "The Myth of Motivation." If your friendships are healthy but you can't stop shopping or eating, head to chapter 8 to learn about habits and addictions. Read what's relevant, skim through the other stuff, and check out the summaries and exercises at the end of each chapter. Ignore the footnotes and return to them when you have time.

Path 3. "I have time. Tell me all the things."

Read through each chapter (in whatever order you want) and do all of the five-minute challenges. Keep a highlighter, pen, and journal nearby. For bonus content, you'll find fun facts and random thoughts in the footnotes. If you find footnotes distracting, you can read each chapter in its entirety first and then go back to the footnotes later. These "brain snacks" are sprinkled throughout the book.

Science . . . or Pseudoscience?

It is a truth universally acknowledged* that the more things we know, the more we come to know that we don't know *anything*.† For example:

- Lightning *can* strike twice.
- Ostriches *don't* bury their heads in the sand to avoid predators.
- The North Star is *not* the brightest star in the sky.
- Bats aren't blind.
- Pluto is *not* a planet.

---

*Modified this phrase from *Pride and Prejudice*. "It is a truth universally acknowledged, that a single man in possession of a good fortune, must be in want of a wife."

†Paraphrase of the original quote attributed to Aristotle: "The more you know, the more you realize you don't know."

Hmm.

Nineteenth-century physicians "canceled" a colleague because he suggested that handwashing reduced mortality in hospitals.* If you googled "biggest living thing on Earth" in early 2021 you'd be told it's the blue whale—but that's inaccurate. The biggest living thing on Earth (as of the time of this writing) is a mushroom in Oregon known as *Armillaria ostoyae*, fondly known as "humongous fungus."

What Does This Mean for You?

When it comes to understanding emotions, behaviors, and consciousness, no one can tell you with absolute certainty, "*This* is how the brain works." The brain is a complex system that is likely unknowable in its entirety. Famed scientist Carl Sagan once wrote: "It has been said that astronomy is a humbling and character-building experience."† The same could be said for neuroscience, considering the cells in your head are no less puzzling and beautiful than a cluster of galaxies. With enough time and research, science *fact* often becomes science *fiction*.

As much as we'd all love to have a stone tablet of unalterable scientific truth, it doesn't exist. This book is a carefully curated compilation of the most helpful information and tools that I've used myself and with clients. It isn't intended to be a "theory of everything" that can be applied to every person for every issue in every circumstance.

---

*Dr. Ignaz Semmelweis's beliefs about handwashing *really* pissed off his colleagues. They didn't like the accusation that their sparkling man-hands needed *more* cleaning before touching patients. Dr. Semmelweis was bullied into a nervous breakdown and he eventually died in a lunatic asylum. Cancel culture is *not* a new concept. See https://www.britannica.com/biography/Ignaz -Semmelweis.

†This Carl Sagan quote comes from *The Pale Blue Dot*. Look up the video if you need a dose of inspiration.

Disclaimer

Science is always subject to change without notice, and researchers on both sides of an issue can cite studies to "prove" just about anything. Because of this, it can be tough to tell the difference between good and bad science. Clashes between science accepters and science deniers often have catastrophic consequences. Examples of this include the debate about whether global warming* is real (it is) and the debate about whether vaccines save lives (they do†). A useful way to approach your process is to ask yourself, *Is believing this idea or trying this exercise going to cause harm to myself or to others?* Much of my work as a psychotherapist is inspired by neat, clean academic theories—but practice is a messier game.

The working assumptions of this book are:

- ▸ When you're in logical mode, it feels like you're in the driver's seat of your brain.
- ▸ When you're in emotional mode, it feels like you're locked in the trunk of a speeding car with no brakes.
- ▸ Your personality is not a singular thing, but a collection of parts and subparts.
- ▸ You have power to change how you *think* (to the degree that you have choices, the willingness to do so, and access to resources).
- ▸ You have power to change how you *act* (to the degree that you have choices, the willingness to do so, and access to resources).

---

*Even skeptics agree that global warming is a real phenomenon. See "Know the Facts: A Skeptic's Guide to Climate Change": https://static.berkeleyearth.org/pdf/skeptics-guide-to-climate-change.pdf.

†Comedian Hannah Gadsby sums it up best in her stand-up special *Douglas*: "As difficult as this life is, it's nice to have a life. And it's particularly nice to have this life in a world without polio. Polio is bad, and that is a fact, not a feeling."

Emotional healing is as much an artistic/creative process as it is a factual/scientific process. Orson Scott Card once wrote: "Metaphors have a way of holding the most truth in the least space." Examples of metaphors used throughout this book, which are *not* intended to be taken literally, include:

- ▸ **Survival Brain:** This is not a literal description of your anatomy.
- ▸ **Limbic System:** Recent discoveries in neuroscience have debunked the idea that there is an exact physiological area where emotions reside.
- ▸ **Hard-Wired Brains:** The brain is a network that constantly changes and evolves. We are not "hard-wired" in the literal sense.
- ▸ **On and Off Brain Switches:** If there were clearly labeled circuits and switches inside our heads, all we'd need to feel better would be brain electricians—not therapists, coaches, or books.

One of the most ubiquitous metaphors you'll see in pop culture (despite its scientific inaccuracy) is the idea you have a "lizard brain." This comes from the (outdated) theory that your brain is a three-layer cake with a bottom layer referred to as the lizard brain, a middle layer termed the emotional brain,* and a top layer called the executive brain. Neuroscientists now tell us the brain is a single network, not a three-layer cake. Research indicates emotions are constructed from your experiences; they're neither preprogrammed nor confined to a specific location of the brain.†

Fair enough. But which of these two statements is more useful to you?

---

* I'll continue to use the terms *emotional brain* and *limbic system* because the word *limbic* comes from the Latin for edge or border. There may not be a literal border that delineates what goes where in the brain, but who among us hasn't felt edgy and irrational?

† "There are no anatomical criteria for deciding which tissue belongs to a 'limbic system' and which does not." https://how-emotions-are-made.com/notes/Criticisms_of_the_limbic_system_concept.

1. "These advances gave birth to the concepts of the ventral striato-pallidal system and extended amygdala, which have changed the way we look at the functional-anatomical organization of the basal forebrain. These discoveries are not easily reconciled with any of the current models of the limbic system."*

OR

2. When you're mad, sometimes it feels like a switch flips in your head causing you to say goodbye to logic brain and hello to angry brain.

You don't *literally* have a demon lizard sitting at the base of your skull who makes you text your ex or yell at your kids.† If you're unfamiliar with the lizard brain theory, watch comedian Iliza Shlesinger's bit about the "party goblin." As she puts it, "your party goblin sleeps in the back of your brain . . . and she will awaken when she hears you say, 'I guess I'll just come out for *one* drink.'" Is the "party goblin" immutable scientific truth—and does it matter? I've directed more than a few clients to Shlesinger's videos because they're funny, relatable, and *helpful*.

When I was neck-deep in sexual dysfunction and drug addiction, digestible doses of information and easy-to-use techniques kept me afloat. What I needed then was what you're holding in your hands now: an assortment of the most potent practices I've collected along my journey. Take what's useful and leave the rest. These remedies can help you feel more empowered with intimacy, friendships, habits, and procrastination. You *don't* have to stay stuck. My own therapist reminded me, "When William James wrote about

---

* https://brainmaster.com/software/pubs/books/Anatomy%20of%20Neuropsychiatry.pdf.

† As of 2020, most neuroscientists no longer support the notion that our lives are ruled by hardwired instincts deployed automatically in response to particular triggers with certain emotions accompanied by a specific facial expression and physical sensation. See https://drsarahmckay.com/rethinking-the-reptilian-brain/.

radical empiricism, he said what's real is what *works*. When you're talking about your emotional health, that's all that really matters."

I'm so glad you're here. Welcome to what will hopefully be a mind-shifting and shame-blasting trip through these pages. I encourage you to speak kindly to yourself and to call a cease-fire on the war in your head. If you feel guilty because "other people have it worse," remember—*perspective* is helpful, but comparison is *not*. You have a right to exist. You have a right to take up space on this planet. You have a right to feel angry, scared, and hurt. And you also have the right to experience happiness in your life and to feel at home in your body.

Let's get unstuck.

CHAPTER 1

Anxiety Is a Superpower

Without It, We Stay Stuck

Madness need not be all breakdown.
It may also be break-through.

—R. D. Laing

When your car's check-engine light flashes, you immediately know it's time to look under the hood. The light itself isn't the problem—it's a signal pointing you *toward* a problem. Trying to "get rid of" anxiety is as counterproductive as trying to disable the check-engine light on your car. In some cases, anxiety is an illness that must be medically managed before anything else can be accomplished. If you're reading this book, however, it's possible that your anxiety is an *indicator light*. Though terrifying, uncomfortable, and confusing, anxiety is actually a superpower that can alter time, leap tall buildings in a single bound, and laser its way through concrete. Most of us learned to view anxiety as an adversary. This chapter will teach you how to view anxiety in a wildly new way.

Why should you believe any of this information when pop psychology headlines tell a different story?

By the time research makes it through the maze of the publishing process, it is already about a decade behind. This is why you'll rarely hear the most current information in mainstream media. Thought leaders such as

Dr. Bessel van der Kolk (*The Body Keeps the Score*), Dr. Stephen Porges (*The Pocket Guide to the Polyvagal Theory*), Dr. Peter Levine (*Waking the Tiger*), and Dr. Pat Ogden (*Trauma and the Body*) have mountains of data showing that mental health requires *body* awareness. Anxiety is one of the physical cues that allow us to know when we are out of alignment with external safety and/or internal truth. Heavy psychotropic medications and labels of mental illness should be the outliers, *not* the norm.

Psychiatrist and trauma authority Dr. Bessel van der Kolk writes: "The past is alive in the form of gnawing interior discomfort . . . in an attempt to control these processes, [people] often become expert at ignoring their gut feelings and in numbing awareness of what is played out inside. They learn to hide from their selves."

> Anxiety is a map that leads you out of stuck.

Since anxiety is a signal, you'll stay stuck without it. I know it feels super-unpleasant, overwhelming, and sometimes even paralyzing to be flooded with anxiety. And yet anxiety is *100 percent* necessary to solve the problem of stuck. Anxiety is *not* an emotion—it's a series of body sensations. Anxiety does not attack you—it's trying to help you. You are *not* crazy or broken if you struggle to manage anxiety.

Wait . . . what?

"But I hate my anxiety!"
"I feel anxious all the time!"
"But my anxiety keeps me from doing things!"
"But my anxiety attacks me!"
"But my anxiety . . ."

FULL STOP.

Most people stare at me like I'm a conspiracy theorist when I explain that anxiety is one of the most important ingredients to getting out of stuck mode. It is clear from the epidemic of panicked, addicted, anxious, overwhelmed, and physically ill people that something is amiss when it comes to our understanding of anxiety. Anxiety doesn't keep you stuck. Anxiety is a map that leads you out of stuck.

According to the Anxiety and Depression Association of America, "anxiety disorders are the most common mental illnesses in the U.S., affecting 40 million adults in the United States . . . or 18.1% of the population every year."

Do 40 million people need to endure a life of incurable mental illness, or is it possible that something else is going on? As a licensed specialist clinical social worker, I am authorized to diagnose you with Generalized Anxiety Disorder, Panic Disorder, Obsessive Compulsive Disorder, Bipolar, and Borderline Personality Disorder by checking your symptoms off a list from the fifth edition of a book called the *Diagnostic and Statistical Manual of Mental Disorders* (DSM-V). The DSM-V* is the bible for mental health professionals. But what most people *don't* know is the DSM is influenced by politicians, it's diagnostically incomplete, and it doesn't take trauma or environmental factors into consideration. My psychopathology professor once told our class, "The DSM should stand for *door-stop manual*, since the only thing it's good for is holding the door open."†

What If the Problem Isn't *Inside* You?

Nowhere in my psychiatric hospital internship was I taught to ask about oppression, patriarchy, or systemic racism as a contributing factor to anxiety. Nowhere in the towering pile of books and assignments was I required to learn about the nervous system, including how the body responds to stress. Nowhere in my first job as a children's therapist did any of the doctors or

---

* Future editions of the DSM will hopefully include more information about trauma and environmental factors.

† Disclaimer: The DSM isn't perfect, but it is necessary. DSM diagnoses allow people access to services and insurance coverage.

therapists look at anxiety as anything other than a medical disease. It is a little-known fact that therapists can become licensed and fully operational without ever learning about the body. I had to do many years of *optional* training (as well as a considerable amount of personal therapy) in order to gather and synthesize the information found in these pages.

Anxiety is not fun. It can sometimes feel life-threatening and disorienting. It makes sense that you've looked outside yourself for answers. But the bright shiny lights *outside* you won't illuminate your understanding. The answers to your questions are found *inside* the dark woods of your own mind. When you try to numb out or avoid anxiety through eating, watching YouTube, comparing yourself to perfect-looking Facebook posts, drinking, or obsessing about relationships, you miss out on powerful signals from your inner world that point you toward your most authentic self. If you learn to listen to its call, anxiety is the shadowy and mysterious guide that can lead you into, through, and safely out of the forest of your chaos. This is a journey many are unwilling to take and others are unable to survive. As M. Scott Peck, who wrote *The Road Less Traveled,* put it, "Mental health is a commitment to reality at all costs."

And sometimes reality feels *really* impossible.

Flashback to my early twenties when I aimlessly swam in a cesspool of stuck. I was living in a cramped Santa Barbara apartment with cigarette butts stuffed to overflowing in piles of empty Diet Coke cans. I was so underweight from anorexia that I stopped having my periods, and when I would try to teach my jam-packed indoor cycling class at Gold's Gym on Monday and Wednesday evenings, I would suddenly begin sweating and shaking, panicked that I'd pass out in front of the crowd of people staring at me. My relational drama was on par with *The Jerry Springer Show*, and I had just come to the realization that my "idyllic childhood" was actually a procession of blurred lines, gaslighting, secrets, and lies—despite everything looking perfectly normal.

After the painful ending of my Santa Barbara adventure, I had no clue what to do with myself. I scraped together the little money I had and fled to a small mountain town in Northern California, where I resolved to understand why I could never seem to slow down, relax, breathe, hear myself think, trust myself, enjoy sex, maintain a relationship, or feel at home in my body. Ultimately I sought refuge in a religious cult. Life was strange but never boring. My daily routine included hours spent in prayer at the missions base, where devotees could be seen splayed out on the floor or pacing up and down the aisles muttering incantations to themselves. After a particularly grueling day of fasting, I grabbed my Bible and a gallon jug of water* (so I could humbly brag to my fellow spiritual warriors that I was choosing to abstain from food and subsist on water) and then sat in my car chain-smoking Marlboro Lights, wondering how in the hell things had devolved into this mess.

New Yorkers aren't exactly known for being easygoing and relaxed. As I entered adolescence in the mid-1990s, anxiety was foremost in the frantic messages from my mother to *watch out for muggers* and in the stern tone my grandmother used when she advised me that "real" ladies should "keep their men happy no matter what." Anxiety imbued what from the outside looked like a normal middle-class family but inside was a roiling mass of boundaryless behavior and distorted parent/child roles. I grew up thinking I was too sensitive, too bossy, too emotional, too needy, too clingy, and too much for my parents to handle. The message I received was to stay small, stay quiet, don't piss off my father, and for god's sake, try not to think so much. After I moved out on my own, anxiety was my constant companion and the antecedent to years of destructive spiritual, sexual, financial, relational, and health choices.

If I had actually opened up to people (I preferred to isolate with my misery back then), I would have told them that if only I could find the right therapist, the right medication, the right program, or the right guru, I would be happy and discover the life I was destined to have. I had no idea what that life might look like, but I knew it would involve being able to eat a meal

---

* A gallon jug of water is a status symbol akin to a Birkin bag in many religious communities. You could carry a regular water bottle like a regular person, but a gallon jug tells everyone you're a food-denying superstar.

without calculating every calorie, being able to sleep without waking up covered in sweat, and being able to look critically at relationships and see red *flags* rather than mistaking them for red *roses*.

You Are Not Broken

The mental health, pharmaceutical, wellness, beauty, and fitness industries are largely built on the idea that anxiety is your fault and "improving yourself" is your solution. Every time you hear an ad promising freedom, joy, bliss, or peace upon purchase of a product or service, you have just fallen prey to the cultural mythology that directs you to look outside yourself for answers. The solutions to many of your problems can be discovered only by journeying within your own mind. For many of my clients, anxiety was the result of *ignoring* themselves, not an indication of a deficiency or brokenness *inside* themselves.

> *Tina was suffering from an eating disorder, obsessive thoughts, and generalized anxiety. Her mother was a controlling, bullying narcissist, but Tina never felt she could say no or set boundaries. Even though she was thirty-two, Tina felt like a six-year-old child anytime she was around her mother. The unending barrage of texts, phone calls, and surprise visits caused Tina to live in a constant state of panic. As a consequence, she lost her boyfriend and her friends, who finally ran out of patience at her refusal to stand up for herself. She was also chronically stuck in jobs for which she was overqualified. Tina repeatedly said, "I know this relationship with my mom is toxic. I know if I could just stand up to her, I could finally be happy, but I just feel so stuck. I just can't. I don't know what's wrong with me."*

Tina's focus on her anxiety was keeping her from seeing the part of herself that was invested in this dysfunction because she was afraid to emotionally step away and make her own decisions. When she faced her fears of growing up, she could finally set boundaries with her mother and courageously take on a challenging and well-paying job in which she ultimately thrived. We'll cover the challenges of adulting in chapter 9.

Naomi came in for vaginismus, which is the most common sexual anxiety problem you've likely never heard of. Vaginismus causes painful constriction and spasms in the vagina anytime penetrative sex or tampon use is attempted. Naomi's husband tried to be compassionate, but he was frustrated and confused by her lack of desire and would often blow up in rages. She was filled with self-loathing and worried that she was going crazy. Nightly panic that her husband would be gone in the morning robbed Naomi of sleep. Though she wanted to be social, she never felt comfortable going out with friends due to a paralyzing fear that her period might start and that her secret would be discovered.

Naomi's anxiety was a signal pointing her toward her dissatisfaction with her marriage. Her husband was an alcoholic with serious anger issues, but the thought of leaving the relationship was terrifying. As a coping mechanism, Naomi's body converted her *psychological* pain into a *physical* problem, a condition known in the mental health world as *conversion disorder.* I've personally struggled with vaginismus, and I can't tell you how many doctors told me it was "all in my head." Their prescriptions were to simply "drink a glass of wine" or to "take some deep breaths." But vaginismus is not a mindset problem—it's a very real *body* problem. While it is *always* necessary to first rule out medical causes with a medical doctor, chronic pain can often be eased or even fully eradicated when uncomfortable emotional truths are faced. When I addressed my sexual trauma, my vaginismus symptoms disappeared. When Naomi came to terms with her desire to be single and took steps toward her truth, she was finally able to enjoy sex and use tampons.

Kaitlyn came into therapy ashamed of her "first-world problems." She had a great job and a perfectly appointed home, and she was held in high regard in the community because of her volunteer work at a local children's hospital. But secretly she drank a bottle of Chardonnay every evening and stayed locked in her room, obliv-

ious to the pleas from her children to play. On the outside she looked perfectly put together, but inside she was falling apart. Kaitlyn was missing deadlines at work and forgetting to show up for important meetings. She believed she was a terrible person for constantly feeling edgy, restless, and irritable. "I have a great husband, beautiful children, a fantastic home—everything a person could want. What is wrong with me that I can't ever seem to relax and enjoy my life? I don't want to be this privileged prissy bitch. Why am I like this?"

Kaitlyn's anxiety and sharp self-talk were an effective distraction from her long-suppressed memories of being screamed at, spanked, and shamed as a child for hiding small animals and live plants in her room, which her mother cruelly threw in the trash or flushed down the toilet anytime little Kaitlyn excitedly tried to sneak them into the house after school. Since she had been raised in a rigid family home where discipline and cleanliness were the laws, she never gave herself permission as an adult to explore creativity or nature. In the course of her therapy, we discovered ways for her to find creative outlets that did not require her to abandon her family, quit her job, or move to a commune. Her symptoms disappeared.

Geri came to therapy because she began having panic attacks after the birth of her second child and felt like a failure as a mom. As much as Geri wanted to keep the house clean, dirty soccer jerseys and muddy jeans covered the floors and crusty dishes filled the sink. As much as she wanted to be the mom who read nightly to her kids, she often shoved the iPad into their hands instead of tucking them into bed. "I feel so stuck with this parenting thing," she said. "I want to be a good mom and I would do anything for my kids, but I just can't seem to be the mom I know they need. What is wrong with me?"

Geri's anxiety was suppressing the taboo but common reality for moms that sometimes motherhood is *really* hard. Since the common perception seems to be that no one is allowed to be publicly overwhelmed by the challenges of parenting, Geri felt like a failure. I've heard from every competent and loving mother I've ever known that while they would die for their kids and do anything for them, a part of them sometimes longs for their pre-motherhood days. There are a few but not nearly enough "parenting stinks sometimes" social media influencers for this phenomenon, even though it is a universal experience. When Geri was able to identify and work through these feelings, her energy returned, her relationship to alcohol was no longer compulsive, and she was able to show up for her life and for her children.

What do Tina, Naomi, Kaitlyn, and Geri have in common? They all believed anxiety was the reason they were stuck. Because the voice of anxiety was far louder than the quiet murmurs from their inner worlds, anxiety commanded the spotlight. But anxiety was the *symptom* of the problem—not the problem itself.

Anxiety Does Not "Attack" You

Calling anxiety an "attack" is like trying to put a fire out with gasoline. If you think there's something inside you that's trying to attack you, your physiology responds as if you were *actually* under attack. We'll talk more about the nervous system in chapter 3. Anxiety *feels* like an attack because it seems to come out of nowhere. When you think that you can be ambushed at any moment, it is challenging to feel safe in your body. But nothing comes from nowhere. Even if you don't know the origin of a symptom, that doesn't mean there isn't a good reason for its being there. Chapter 3 will discuss what to do when you don't know why your body is freaking out and how to help yourself—even if you have no clue why you're triggered. The way we've been taught to deal with anxiety clearly does not work, evidenced by the millions of people in the United States affected by mental illness each year. The compulsive avoidance of and misconceptions about anxiety lead to emotional havoc and profound unhappiness.

I remember sitting on the floor of a restorative yoga class and having a meltdown when instructed to put my legs up on the wall. *What is wrong with you? Get it together!* I scolded myself. This class was the epitome of Zen relax-

ation: soft music, dim lights, pillows and blankets, and comfortable body posi-
tions. Yet I was shaking, my palms were sweating, and it took every ounce of
willpower I could summon to keep from running out the door. Since I made a
habit of ignoring my feelings, the effort to force relaxation on my system triggered my internal alarm. My anxiety, sensing I was finally moving slowly
enough to hear myself think, screamed, "YOU ARE NOT OKAY!" Though
deep breathing can be useful and isn't inherently bad, anyone who has ever
tried (and failed) to reduce anxiety through meditation, self-care, breathing,
bubble baths, or yoga knows that something else is needed to get unstuck.

What Is the "Something Else"?

The human brain is powerful, beautiful, and mysterious. Current research
indicates that we are wired for survival,* not happiness. We are wired to
seek safety, not serenity. This means that your brain is constantly scanning
your environment in search of threats and opportunities. But since you no
longer live in a cave or in the presence of lions, tigers, and bears, your brain is
prone to misinterpreting danger cues. The impact of this confusion on your
well-being is staggering. Even though you logically know you are safe, it often feels impossible to get yourself moving. When your brain operates in
survival mode, you might feel overwhelmed, reactive, impulsive, hostile, and
simultaneously wired and exhausted. Loved ones instantly become hostile
predatory animals.

The technical term for this experience is *neuroception*—the brain's perception of people, places, and things as safe or dangerous. An inaccurate read on
safety as opposed to danger is a breeding ground for debilitating symptoms
and disastrous relationships. A neuroception of danger will create the *exact*
same symptoms as an anxiety disorder. But these symptoms are *survival*

---

* *Survival* refers to physical safety and efficient management of energy needs.

responses—not disorders or diseases. Anytime you are anxious, it is likely that you've switched out of rational mode and into survival mode. When you are intentional, decisive, and mindful, the activity in the logical part of the brain feels like it's lit up. When you are reactive, out of control, and stuck, that's because you've left "logic land" and entered the realm of *survival brain*.

Survival brain is not designed to harm you. The language we *all* learned to use is inaccurate—a panic attack is not an attack. A panic attack is your brain's misinterpretation of data. A panic attack is your brain trying to be helpful and keep you safe. Most people are taught to believe the following myths about anxiety:

> A panic attack is not an attack.

- ▸ It's a disease.
- ▸ It's a chemical imbalance.
- ▸ It's a genetic issue.
- ▸ It's a mental disorder.
- ▸ It's a sign of mental weakness.

Myth: Anxiety is a disease.

Consequences of believing this myth: "If it's a disease, then I just have to learn to live with it."

The disease model of mental health is useful because it gives people access to mental health services and insurance coverage. But when you refer to anxiety as a disease, you'll likely feel even more helpless and overwhelmed. Anxiety is not intended to hurt you but to *help* you if you're unsafe or veering away from authenticity. Limping after you twist your ankle isn't a disease—the pain is a signal that an injury needs attention. Vomiting after taking tequila shots isn't a disease, but a signal that you've had too much to drink. Instead of viewing anxiety as a disease, look at it as a signal; this is a more effective framework for getting unstuck.

Myth: Anxiety is a chemical imbalance.

Consequences of believing this myth: "All I need is medication."

The chemical imbalance theory is a *theory*, not a fact. The drugs that are promoted to treat anxiety (and depression*) can cause addiction, dependence, and side effects. Benzodiazepines (benzos) are a class of drugs for anxiety that include Xanax, Ativan, Klonopin, and Valium. These drugs, if used occasionally, can serve to address isolated bouts of panic or occasional events such as long plane rides or dangerous PTSD (post-traumatic stress disorder) flashbacks. However, these medications are highly addictive, and all too often patients are not informed about the risks. Medications are useful and definitely have their place, but without knowing all the information and possible alternatives, many people find that the cure ends up being worse than the symptoms. (My disclaimer here is to remind everyone that your wellness is *your* choice, and for some people, medications are miracles.)

Full disclosure? I take psychiatric medication. This is *not* because I took a blood test that showed a dopamine or serotonin "imbalance." Why do I take them? After a *lot* of trial and error (including a hospitalization from a severe allergic reaction to bipolar meds), I found a medication that helps to round out my jagged edges. If taking meds helps you to feel *more* like yourself, great. That's why I take them. The point of psych meds is to help you (safely) *feel* your feelings—not to *escape* from your feelings. If you are not a medication person, make sure you speak to your doctor before making changes. Either way, in order to make fully informed choices, you must be aware of the potential dangers of psychiatric medications and the inaccuracy of the chemical imbalance theory.

Chris, a client referred to me by a local doctor, was on such a high dose of

*Ana Florence, "Disproven Chemical Imbalance Theory Leads to Worse Depression Outcomes." Open Excellence, August 4, 2020. https://openexcellence.org/disproven-chemical-imbalance-theory-leads-to-worse-depression-outcomes/.

Xanax that they couldn't speak without slurring, yet had *no* idea this symptom was directly caused by their medication. Their doctor never once explained this to them. I myself was personally prescribed Ativan for my anxiety, and no one ever explained the addictive properties of the drug. Too many people are unaware of the very high cost they might pay for a few hours of benzo-induced relief. Believing the chemical imbalance theory leads sufferers to believe that the origin of their problems is purely chemical. A simple Google search will produce countless experts who speak to the inaccuracy of the chemical imbalance theory.* Our brains are highly intricate systems and there is no simple way (as of today) to clearly pinpoint what a "chemically balanced" brain looks like. "Chemical imbalance is sort of last-century thinking. It's much more complicated than that," neuroscientist Joseph Coyle of Harvard Medical School was quoted as saying in a blog by National Public Radio's Alix Spiegel.

Myth: Anxiety is a genetic issue.

Consequences of believing this myth: "There is nothing I can do about it."

Are genes important to consider? Yes. But environment is an equally important factor in the anxiety equation. There is no way to identify a singular cause of anxiety. Genes may explain some of your tendencies, but your genetic code does not define you. Some people use the "anxiety is genetic" explanation to avoid the change process. Granted, the change process can be painful, and most of us (myself included) prefer to avoid pain. In his fascinating book on epigenetics,† author Mark Wolynn writes:

---

* "DSM definitions do not include personal and contextual factors such as whether the depressive symptoms are an understandable response to loss, a terrible life situation, psychological conflict or personality factors." Allen Frances, *Saving Normal: An Insider's Revolt Against Out -of-Control Psychiatric Diagnosis, DSM-5, Big Pharma, and the Medicalization of Ordinary Life.*

† Per the CDC, "Epigenetics is the study of how your behaviors and environment can cause changes that affect the way your genes work. Unlike genetic changes, epigenetic changes are reversible and do not change your DNA sequence, but they can change how your body reads a DNA sequence." https://www.cdc.gov/genomics/disease/epigenetics.htm.

When we try to resist feeling something painful, we often protract the very pain we're trying to avoid. Doing so is a prescription for continued suffering. There's also something about the action of searching that blocks us from what we seek. The constant looking outside of ourselves can keep us from knowing when we hit the target. Something valuable can be going on inside us, but if we're not tuning in, we can miss it.*

In other words, genes are not a reason to accept anxiety or other mental health issues as inescapable and set in stone.

Myth: Anxiety is a mental disorder.

Consequences of believing this myth: "There is something wrong with me."

After canceling her previous two sessions with no notice, Jan, a forty-two-year-old graphic designer, returned to my office a few weeks later looking and sounding exhausted. After a long period of abstinence from bulimia symptoms, Jan found herself once again spending most of her days locked in a cycle of bingeing and purging. "I don't know what's wrong with me," she said. "I just feel so anxious all the time and it comes out of absolutely nowhere."

The idea that anxiety "comes out of nowhere" is a common complaint from anxiety sufferers and contributes to the myth that anxiety is a mental disorder. A quick brain hack to halt a panic episode is to tell yourself over and over again, "It didn't come from nowhere. . . . There's a reason for this even if I don't know what it is." It can be comforting to remind yourself that all symptoms make sense in context—even if you don't know the context. Nothing comes out of "nowhere." Anxiety *always* has an origin.

---

*Mark Wolynn, *It Didn't Start with You*. My caveat about this book is that while there is plenty of helpful information, I disagree with Wolynn's theory that you need to reconcile with and forgive your parents. Forgiveness is a beautiful gift—but it is *not* required to heal from trauma.

For Jan, bulimia was an effective distraction from her high-conflict divorce and out-of-control teenager. Bulimia (and other eating disorders) can be deadly. Eating disorder symptoms need to be medically managed before any psychological work can have an impact. However, eating disorders are not illnesses that exist in a vacuum. Most trauma-informed therapists use a systems approach to eating disorders. Systems theory believes that behavior is shaped by a complex network of factors. These factors—including home environment, work, school, genetics, and economic status—function together as a system to influence decisions and outcomes.

In *The Myth of Mental Illness*, the late professor of psychiatry at the State University of New York Upstate Medical University and a distinguished lifetime fellow of the American Psychiatric Association Thomas Szasz wrote: "Psychiatric assessment too often fails to appreciate personal and social precursors of mental illness by avoiding or not taking into account such psychosocial considerations. Mainstream psychiatry acts on the somatic hypothesis of mental illness to the detriment of understanding people's problems."

An illness or disorder is defined as something going wrong in the mind or body. We need to ask not what is *wrong* with anxiety but what is *right* about it. If anxiety is looked at as a disorder or illness, then every single attempt to fix it will fail. Anxiety does not need to be "fixed"—it needs to be understood. Why? When you look closely at the factors surrounding your anxiety, you'll be surprised to discover that your "overreactions" and "meltdowns" actually make *total* sense in context.

> Anxiety does not need to be "fixed"—it needs to be understood.

Myth: Anxiety is a sign of mental weakness.

Consequence of believing this myth: "I am broken."

The presence of anxiety means that your brain and body are doing exactly what they are designed to do, which is to indicate danger or to highlight when you are ignoring a vital message. It is a sign of *strength* to feel anxiety. Many of my clients initially balk at the notion that feeling like an anxious wreck is a sign of strength. But it takes a herculean amount of strength to tolerate the feeling of anxiety—and an even greater amount of courage to listen to the *message* of anxiety. With instant access to Instagram, Hulu, and 24/7 news cycles, not to mention the availability of Ketel One, Tinder, blackjack, and handcrafted Etsy jewelry, certainly we find it more convenient than ever before to run from the quiet inner voice of truth.

It is not a sign of strength to be numb. It is not a sign of weakness to feel emotional pain. Though you may initially jump at the chance to never feel pain, there is a severe consequence when you disconnect from your pain receptors. The inability to feel pain is not a gift. In fact, the inability to feel pain is a symptom of the debilitating illness Hansen's disease, or what many people call *leprosy*. Leprosy is a nerve condition that disables the pain response. Without pain, you'd never know if a stove is hot, if a knife is sharp, or if you're scratching an itch too hard. If you turn off your ability to feel physical pain, the consequence is literal death. If you try to turn off your ability to feel emotional pain, the consequence is *emotional* death.

> It is not a sign of weakness to feel emotional pain.

Anxiety, Fear, and Worry— What's the Difference?

People often use the words *anxiety*, *fear*, and *worry* interchangeably. These three words are similar but not synonymous. Imagine the epic Pinterest fails you'd produce if you believed sugar, salt, and flour were all the same. There are significant differences between anxiety, fear, and worry. Let's consider the case of Jo, thirty-four, a client who came to therapy for social anxiety.

Anxiety

As I pointed out earlier in the chapter, anxiety is like the check-engine light on your car. The check-engine light doesn't always identify specific problems, it simply cues you to take your car in for service.* Anxiety is a series of uncomfortable physical sensations in your body without an identifiable source. Anxiety is a trail that leads to unaddressed emotional injuries. Jo didn't know why she felt anxious in social settings, so she assumed there was something wrong with her. She was so focused on her "anxiety attacks" she didn't realize there was a *function* to these feelings. Rather than following the trail to its source, Jo was stuck in shame and self-blame.

Fear

Fear shows up in the body with the same physical sensations as anxiety: shallow breathing, rapid heart rate, sweaty palms, dry mouth, and tension. But unlike anxiety, fear is tied to a direct source. Sometimes the source is a present danger and sometimes it is a future concern. Jo's dilemma was not social anxiety. What was the real problem? Social situations unconsciously reminded her of the college frat party where she experienced a sexual assault. Jo's problem wasn't a mental illness—it was *unresolved trauma*. Her body produced a *fear response* when faced with social situations. Because Jo believed she should be over the incident and that it "wasn't really that bad," she buried her feelings. These buried feelings announced their existence as a fear response in social situations—particularly in social situations where men outnumbered women.

Worry

Worry is diet fear. Fear lite. Worry creates the same body cues as fear but without the intensity. After Jo realized her social anxiety was a completely

---

* Some cars do have check-engine lights that report specific problems. If only it were that simple for anxiety.

reasonable fear, our next task was to turn her fear into a *worry*. Managing a worry feels way more doable than trying to "get over" a fear. Jo was worried about getting stuck in dangerous situations. This worry made total sense in context, so she no longer felt crazy. Since she could now think clearly without the weight of shame, Jo decided to stand near the exit doors during social events. Her logic brain turned back on and we brainstormed a list of coping strategies, including frequently checking in with a supportive friend, validating the pain from her past, and giving herself permission to leave events early. Eventually she was able to completely eliminate her "social anxiety."

Final Thoughts

Anxiety attacks are not really attacks. It would be more accurate to call them episodes. The language you use to describe your experiences has a huge impact on your ability to change your experiences. Your body is not trying to hurt you. When you realize your body is actually on your side, you no longer fear anxiety episodes or feel as much shame and guilt. When shame and guilt are removed from the equation, it is astounding how quickly you can find your way to workable solutions. Anxiety is sometimes the result of ignoring yourself. Anxiety is sometimes the result of threats outside yourself. Anxiety is not a result of anything defective inside yourself.

Anxiety disorders should be called anxiety responses instead. You are *not* crazy.

BOTTOM-LINE TAKEAWAYS

1. Anxiety is like the check-engine light on your car. If you disable it, you're screwed.
2. Your brain is wired to keep you alive—*not* to keep you happy.
3. A panic attack is not an attack. It is your brain trying to talk to you.
4. The inability to feel pain is not strength—it's emotional leprosy.
5. Anxiety is *not* a disease.

6. Anxiety always comes from somewhere—even if you don't know where that *somewhere* is.

7. The chemical imbalance theory of depression has never been proven.*

8. Anxiety does not need to be fixed—it needs to be *understood*.

9. A survival response will often look like an anxiety disorder, but it isn't.

10. You are not crazy.

DOS AND DON'TS

Do	Don't
Tell yourself, "Just because I don't know why I'm feeling like this doesn't mean there's not a *really* good reason for these feelings to be here."	Shame yourself by saying things like "What's wrong with me?"
Remind yourself that your body is not attacking you. It is trying to help you.	Minimize how badly you feel. Even though anxiety is a helpful mechanism, it is still awful and terrifying.
Ask yourself if there are areas of your life you hesitate to address because you fear the outcome.	Feel like you have to deal with everything at once. If numbing out safely helps you make it through the day, enabling you to take care of your responsibilities, you're allowed to numb. We all need a numb-out session periodically.
Talk to your doctor about medications and make sure you understand the full range of possible side effects—including the potential for dependency.	Decide to stop medication without talking to your doctor. Medication can be a lifesaver for some people in some situations.

---

* At this current time, the chemical imbalance theory hasn't been proven.

FIVE-MINUTE CHALLENGES

1. On one side of a piece of paper, list all the stressful people in your
   life. Don't worry about hurting their feelings—this is for your
   eyes only. On the other side of the paper, for each person listed,
   write: *My* real *feelings about him/her/them are* _____.
   At the bottom, write: *I have a right to my feelings*.

2. Make a list of all the stressful tasks on your plate. At the bottom,
   write: *It makes sense that I'm feeling overwhelmed. I'll feel much better
   when I do* _____ *first*.

3. Make a list of anything else that is stressing you out (physical illness, oppressive work environment, financial burdens, etc.). At
   the bottom, write five things that you can do in the next five
   minutes to make you feel 5 percent less stressed.

4. Write a note to yourself that says, *My anxiety makes sense—anyone
   in this situation would feel anxious. I may not be able to understand it
   all or change it all right now—but I know without a doubt that I am
   not crazy*. Put the note where you can see it daily.

CHAPTER 2

The Hidden Benefits of Staying Stuck

We can talk about courage and love and compassion until we
sound like a greeting card store, but unless we're willing to have
an honest conversation about what gets in the way of putting
these into practice in our daily lives, we will never change.
Never, ever.

—Brené Brown, *The Gifts of Imperfection*

When I ask clients why they think they're stuck, I hear the same
responses:

"I'm just so lazy."

"I have no motivation."

"There's something wrong with me."

"I just can't seem to get going."

"I'm broken."

"I'm crazy."

"I'm not good enough."

"They will reject me if I try."

Brené Brown taught us that embedded within our imperfections are
gifts. In *Daring Greatly*, she writes: "Because true belonging only happens
when we present our authentic, imperfect selves to the world, our sense of
belonging can never be greater than our level of self-acceptance."

Dr. Brown's work launched a self-acceptance revolution. If there are gifts in your imperfections, surely there are also gifts to be found in your stuck-ness. What kind of gifts could possibly be unearthed from the states of stuck that you are so quick to judge? Sometimes there are subconscious rewards for staying stuck. These rewards incentivize you to remain exactly where you are, how you are, and who you are. When you can examine your motivations and biases with ferocious self-*acceptance* rather than relentless self-*shame*, your capacity to mobilize in the direction of your dreams expands.

Even the most traumatic environments can lure us into inaction with their siren songs. I remember the first time I was hit over the head with this realization. In my midtwenties, I was working as an associate producer for a television network you've never heard of on a reality show you've never seen. After drifting aimlessly across the country working as a seafood res-taurant hostess, a steak-house waitress, a photo shoot coordinator, a free-lance magazine writer, and a basement organizer, I found a job at a television production company. I wrangled lots of praise and many pats on the back for my ability to make people cry on-camera, a skill of which I was not proud.

My alarm went off at three A.M., insisting with its ear-numbing screech that I peel the stiff blanket off my protesting body and get to work. I splashed some water on my face, chain-smoked a few cigarettes, and downed a tepid twenty-ounce gas station coffee. Then I headed toward the Las Vegas Strip. My job for the next sixteen hours would be to run around with a camera crew gathering footage for a show about abusive relationships. The women fea-tured in this project understood *stuck* better than any people I've worked with prior to or since. And in our conversations, they disclosed a surprising truth I've heard echoed again and again from a diverse group of people.

What Was the Surprising Truth?

Here's that truth: If you dig under most unhealthy behaviors, you'll find hid-den rewards. Every single woman I interviewed affirmed they received plenty of rewards, especially in the beginning of their relationships. Many of the women spoke with wistful longing about their initial years with abusive partners. Dreamy glazed eyes and half-smiles often appeared on their battle-weary faces when they described the "good" times. To an outside observer, it seems impossible that violent relationships could offer any rewards. And yet all the interviewees reported feeling (initially) very happy. Even when their partners turned on them, these women reported that the allure of rewards kept them returning again and again.

If it was easy for those in abusive relationships to leave, we would all do it. As any gambler can attest, the promise of a reward creates a cycle of repetition. These women felt stuck because they were afraid to start over. They believed they needed a white knight to come and rescue them—a myth that many women, including me, fall prey to believing. As someone who has been stuck in a violent relationship, I understand the fear of starting over. I understand the desire to outsource the job of rescuer. I also understand how even the most traumatic and abusive relationships provide rewards. If I'm being brutally honest, I'll admit I tolerated toxic behaviors in exchange for the rewards of community esteem, financial security, and companionship. But while many domestic violence survivors stay in dangerous relationships, abuse is never, ever, *ever* the fault of the person being abused. *No one* gets to say, "You deserved to be abused because you chose to stay and receive the hidden benefits." NO.

While these examples are extreme, everyone—including you—receives rewards from "unhealthy" behaviors. In order to get unstuck, you must take an honest inventory of your behaviors—even the ones that I know you genuinely wish to change. Shaming yourself and bemoaning your choices won't work. Instead of judging your behavior, you need to get curious about it. Curiosity is fuel for the change process. When you can observe your behaviors with curiosity, it's easier to see their benefits. Understanding the function of a behavior is the key to changing it. When I talk about the hidden benefits of unhealthy behaviors, one skeptic in the group always raises a hand and says, "Wait—are we supposed to actually believe that there are health benefits to being a couch potato/chronic procrastinator?"

Yes. That is exactly what I'm saying. Allow me to elaborate.

Our brains are wired for survival, not happiness. Our nervous systems are trained to conserve as much energy as possible. Staying stuck is an efficient use of resources when the goal is *survival*. Staying stuck is problematic when the goal is *productivity*. Understanding the perks of staying stuck is the first step toward change.

Perks of Staying Stuck—The Four P's

There are four important perks to consider:

- **Prevents** discomfort
- **Protects** you from emotions
- **Promotes** connection
- **Points** to problems

Prevents Discomfort

Staying stuck is a way to stay comfortable. We feel warm and cozy when we huddle under the covers. If we stay stuck, we prevent the discomfort that accompanies the change process. It takes courage to examine the chaos beneath the glass-smooth waters of our public personas. Often, when you take a fearless and thorough inventory of your relationships, career, habits, and beliefs, you'll discover that getting unstuck requires uncomfortable conversations. If you're concerned that making changes could shake up your status quo, then you will be unconsciously invested in staying stuck.

Irina, a bubbly fifty-two-year-old, came into my office armed with a notebook full of charts, lists, and timelines of her anxiety symptoms. In her bag she carried several personal growth books and a multi-page inventory of supplements and medications from her doctor that were intended to "cure her anxiety disorder." As I gently worked to tease out her story, she tentatively admitted she was unhappy in her job. "BUT," she stated emphatically through her red-rimmed glasses, "it's a really good job and they take good care of me. I've worked for the company for thirteen years, and if I left, I'd have to start all over again. I don't want to talk about my work situation. I just really need to focus on this anxiety and find a way to stop my panic attacks." Irina had a paralyzing fear of being a quitter and was therefore unwilling to look at the reality of her toxic work environment—she was overworked, underpaid, and constantly dodging inappropriate comments from her mansplaining supervisor. One of the benefits of Irina's situation was maintaining a facade of loyalty and consistency. She was worried that if she committed to the process of getting unstuck, she would realize how miserable she was feeling in her job and would have to leave.

Protects You from Emotions

There are no negative emotions. There are uncomfortable and scary emotions, but even our most unpleasant emotions have an important function. Anger points to injustice. Sadness points to loss. Fear points to threat. Staying stuck is a way to avoid distressing emotions. Emotions can feel uncomfortable, frightening, and confusing. I had to become thoroughly sick of spacing out in conversations, finding myself in abusive relationships, and feeling shame when I looked at my body in the mirror. Only then was I willing to face my emotions. Until you believe that getting unstuck will be worth the fear of facing your emotions, you'll continue to stay stuck.

Promotes Connection

My mother's mother died suddenly from a brain aneurysm, after which her father left her to be raised by abusive relatives. My mother was two. Anxiety permeated her system at that point, and she's been stuck ever since. If your primary attachment figure is stuck in a state of high anxiety, they are not emotionally available to fully engage with you. Since they can't create a secure attachment, you will try to connect by mimicking their behaviors. As a child, I was highly sensitive, nervous, and clingy. Subconsciously I was trying to bond with my mother by sharing her anxiety. These early attachment issues resulted in a chronic sense of disconnection and unworthiness. Unless parented properly, little kids believe that they are bad if they don't act like their parents. We'll talk more about attachment and family dynamics in chapter 7.

Points to Problems

People often use the word *depressed* interchangeably with the word *stuck*. Clinical depression has historically been thought of as a medical disease, but research about trauma and the brain offers an alternative perspective. Clinical psychologist Dr. Phil Hickey* writes:

> Contrary to the APA's assertion, depression is not an illness. In fact, depression is an adaptive mechanism which has served humanity well for millions of years. When things are going well in our lives, we feel good. This good feeling is nature's way of telling us to keep doing what we are doing. When our lives are not going well, we feel down or depressed. This is nature's way of telling us to make some changes.

As someone who has suffered with clinical depression for years, when exposed to this alternative viewpoint, I thought: *Wait . . . what? Depression is NOT a disease? Try telling that to anyone who has ever felt like dying, like disappearing, or to someone who couldn't get out of bed for weeks.*

The symptoms of depression are very real and often life-threatening. When you understand the brain's shutdown mechanism† (discussed more in-depth in the next chapter), space is created for a more empowering lens with which to view depression. Depression is not always an internal sickness.

---

*Phil Hickey, "Depression Is Not an Illness: It Is an Adaptive Mechanism." *Behaviorism and Mental Health*, March 9, 2013. https://www.behaviorismandmentalhealth.com/2009/07/28/depression/.

†The brain's shutdown mechanism is explained in detail in chapter 3. None of this information should be taken as medical advice or therapy. Often depression symptoms must be medically managed before any psychological interventions can have an impact.

Even if everything looks fine on the surface, a brain that feels safe will *not* usually produce symptoms of clinical depression. Depression is often a signal pointing *to* a problem, not the problem itself. Anxiety and depression may seem like they play for different teams, but they both serve the same purpose. While environmental circumstances can make it difficult or even impossible to heal from anxiety and depression, these brain states are not out to get you. Both anxiety and depression are efforts by your brain to protect you from harm. Is depression a disease? Maybe. But a tongue-in-cheek anonymous quote I see often on social media highlights an important disclaimer: "Before you diagnose yourself with depression or low self-esteem, first make sure that you are not, in fact, just surrounded by assholes."

Top Nine Benefits of Staying Stuck

1. **Energy conservation:** If you don't do things, you don't have to expend valuable energy doing things.
2. **Image preservation:** If you keep yourself stuck, you don't have to worry about people finding out you're a "fraud."
3. **Risk management:** If you don't start doing things, you don't have to worry about failing at things.
4. **Control:** If you keep your ideas safely confined to your head, you can maintain control over them.
5. **Pain numbing:** If you never start doing things, you can numb out by fantasizing about "someday" doing things.
6. **Familiarity:** We often accept the discomfort of the familiar rather than risk the unknown of change—even positive change.
7. **Safety:** Sometimes it feels safer to stay small.
8. **Financial security:** Staying stuck doesn't require you to risk resources for an unknown outcome.
9. **Relationship equilibrium:** If you don't do things, you don't have to worry about shifting the dynamic of your relationships.

> Procrastination is not laziness.

Willingness to admit to the benefits of your choices creates forward momentum. Denying the benefits of your choices fosters shame. Procrastination is a great example of how an "unhealthy" behavior provides benefits. Procrastination is not laziness. Procrastination is a form of protection that keeps you from face-planting into shame. If you never actually complete that project, apply for that job, go on that date, or start that exercise program, you'll never have to risk failure and rejection. Whether you want to get fit, cultivate meaningful connections with people, start a business, jump into the dating pool, or bring a creative dream to fruition, the benefits of staying stuck are numerous.

None of this information is a call to stop taking medications (never do that without talking to your doctor). This information is *not* intended to minimize or discredit your pain—your symptoms are real, your pain is real, and your depression and anxiety are also real. Sometimes our most extreme symptoms need to be managed medically before we attempt any psychological interventions. That said, feeling stuck is a *survival response*. We'll discuss survival responses in more detail in chapter 3. A brain stuck in survival mode will exhibit the same symptoms as clinical depression, but these are *not* the same.

When Talking Doesn't Work

Julie, a client who suffered from crippling panic episodes and psychological nonepileptic seizures (seizures brought on by emotional and not medical causes), found healing simply by learning to befriend and understand survival responses. She went from fifteen to twenty seizures a day to zero. The first thing Julie needed to do was stop blaming herself. She'd berate herself and say, "I hate that my brain is so weak. Why can't I just stop doing this? I need it to stop!" Imagine yelling this at an infant and expecting the baby to understand:

"I hate that you are so weak. Why can't you stop crying? Stop crying this instant!"

It would look and seem ridiculous (not to mention abusive) because babies do not have the capacity to understand your thoughts or your words. Thinking and talking about the problem did not help Julie solve the problem. Why? The part of your brain often referred to as the limbic (emotional) system does not respond to logic or to positive thinking. It is not your fault if you struggle to talk or think your way out of stuck. Thinking about problems helps only if your thinking brain is available. Using your thoughts and words to solve your problems is the main idea behind cognitive behavioral therapy (CBT).

Cognitive behavioral therapy is an evidence-based approach to mental health. This model attempts to use logical thinking to reduce distressing feelings. CBT definitely has its place. A 2018 article in *Frontiers in Psychology* states: "Because of its clear research support, CBT dominates the international guidelines for psychosocial treatments, making it a first-line treatment for many disorders."*

AND.

This same journal article also states: "Having said that, we must add that, although CBT is efficacious/effective, there is still room for improvement, as in many situations there are patients who do not respond to CBT and/or relapse. . . . Therefore we predict continuous improvements in psychotherapy will derive from CBT, gradually moving the field toward an integrative scientific psychotherapy."

CBT has limitations. One of its major limitations is that the model doesn't train people to understand how their *bodies* contribute to thoughts and feelings. There are *body-based* reasons why your thoughts don't always succeed in changing your feelings. Julie struggled to manage her seizures be-

---

*Daniel David, Ioana Cristea, and Stefan G. Hofmann, "Why Cognitive Behavioral Therapy Is the Current Gold Standard of Psychotherapy." *Frontiers in Psychiatry* 9 (2018): 4. https://doi.org/10.3389/fpsyt.2018.00004.

cause she tried to use a mind-based solution for a body-based problem. CBT is a mind-based solution that uses the power of *thoughts* to change *feelings*. Body-based therapies use the power of *feelings* to change *thoughts*. We need both. Once you can get your "logic brain" back online, then you will find use for cognitive tools like positive thinking, affirmations, and encouraging self-talk. We'll talk more about body-based solutions later in this chapter.

Feelings, Emotions, and Thoughts— What's the Difference?

Accurately naming your experiences is the first step toward changing your experiences. If you don't know how to properly describe something, any intervention you attempt is likely to fall flat. If you go to the emergency room and fail to describe your symptoms accurately, you might end up receiving an appendectomy when what you actually need is antibiotics for a bladder infection. One major contributor to staying stuck is not knowing the difference between feelings, emotions, and thoughts. These are not the same. Learning to identify, examine, and separate them can produce incredible changes in mood and an overall sense of well-being. The mental health world does a great disservice to people when it uses the words *feelings*, *emotions*, and *thoughts* interchangeably. Let's break this down.

Feelings

Feelings are a series of *body sensations*. Feelings are purely *physical*. If you are tired, you might report feelings of heavy eyelids, a lack of energy, and sleepiness. Anxiety is a *feeling* because it is a cluster of body sensations such as a racing heart, sweaty palms, a dry mouth, and a tight chest. Pain is a *feeling* because it is a series of body sensations. Tight, loose, buzzy, dizzy, cold, hot, tired . . . These are all feelings.

Why does this matter? In order to slow your brain down enough to get back into a rational brain state, you need to take your interpretations and emotions *out* of the equation and first focus strictly on the body cues/feelings. Telling yourself, *There has to be something wrong with me*, is an interpretation. It's a story. Telling yourself, *I should be able to manage this*, is also a story. When you attach *stories* to *symptoms*, you stay *stuck*. Simplification is the first step to finding relief.

When someone comes into my office loaded with emotions and stories, the first question I ask them is "Where are you feeling these things in your body?" When you pull your attention away from stories and emotions and focus first on body sensations, the feelings of overwhelm often immediately lessen in intensity. Why? The act of observing your experience changes your experience.

Emotions

Emotions are body sensations with a *story* attached to them. On Tuesday, you might experience the body sensations of a tense jaw, clenched fists, and a racing heart. This might feel like anger, since your story is that you didn't get the promotion you wanted. On Saturday, you might experience the same feelings of a tense jaw, clenched fists, and a racing heart. But instead of experiencing these feelings as anger, you experience them as excitement, because you're about to start that half-marathon you've been training for all summer. The difference between Tuesday's anger and Saturday's excitement is your story.

Feelings + Stories = Emotions. It is the stories we attach to our body sensations that create emotions.

You would not break your ankle and call the resulting pain an emotion. You would not describe stomach cramps as an emotion. These are feelings. Why does this matter? Feeling stuck can be terrifying because it's a free-floating series of body sensations onto which we project stories of shame and *inadequacy*. When you view symptoms as concrete and physiological, rather than as abstract or ethereal, they become much easier to contain and therefore

Feelings +
Stories =
Emotions

reduce. When I work with overwhelmed clients, my immediate goal is to help them take the broad concept of stuckness and turn it into something tangible. How does this work? Let's take the example of Maddie, a twenty-nine-year-old client. When she came in for a session, Maddie began sweating and hyperventilating the moment she sat down.

> Maddie: *I feel like I'm going crazy. I'm so anxious right now I feel like I'm going to die, and I'm so mad at myself for still feeling this way. What's wrong with me?*
>
> Me: *You feel really overwhelmed right now. Can you tell me where in your body you feel anxious?*
>
> Maddie: *I feel tightness in my chest and my heart is beating really fast.*
>
> Me: *Are you willing to focus on the tightness in your chest?*
>
> Maddie: *Yes.*
>
> Me: *Great. Tell me about the qualities you notice about the tightness. Does it have a color or a shape?*
>
> Maddie: *It feels like a big ball of red.*
>
> Me: *Does that big ball of red have a size? Can you locate where it begins and ends?*
>
> Maddie: *It feels like it's the size of a grapefruit. It starts right below my throat and ends in the middle of my chest.*
>
> Me: *Can you put your hand on the area in your body where you feel this? What do you think that grapefruit-sized ball would need from you right now if it could talk?*
>
> Maddie: *I think it would need me to slow down and try to take care of it.*
>
> Me: *Is slowing down and taking care of it something that makes sense to you?*
>
> Maddie: *Well, actually . . . yes. This week has been insane. I haven't been able to do my usual workouts or meal planning because my mother isn't doing well. I think she's going to need to go into assisted living, and with COVID-19 . . .*

From there, Maddie was able to calm down enough to flip her logic switch back on. At that point, we could process her thoughts about her mother's health situation and come up with a strategy for coping with the stresses of caregiving. As she brought her attention toward the sensations, the panic settled down and she could think clearly. When we talked about the health benefits of staying stuck, Maddie was surprised to realize that *energy* was one of the benefits of her anxiety. "When I really stopped to think about it," she admitted, "I was afraid that if I stopped feeling so buzzy, then depression would take over and I wouldn't be able to do anything at all. Anxiety is awful, but it does give you lots of energy."

It's important to examine your beliefs about and the benefits of your behavior. Instead of shaming yourself for feeling stuck, look for stories. In Maddie's case, once we identified the feelings in her chest and recognized her need to recommit herself to her self-care, her story that she was crazy ended up shifting. She learned to tell herself, *Of course I feel overwhelmed. I haven't taken care of myself and I have a mountain of responsibility on me. This is starting to make sense.*

When you mix up thoughts, feelings, and emotions, it becomes impossible to do the exploration necessary to reach solutions. This would be like trying to find your way through a national park with no trail markers and with debris obstructing the path. In Maddie's case, when we took the stories ("I'm going crazy") and the emotions ("I'm so mad at myself") out of the equation and focused first on the feelings (tight chest), the pieces became easier to organize.

Thoughts

Thoughts are mental constructs such as ideas, beliefs, perspectives, opinions, and judgments. Thoughts may or may not have accompanying body sensations. You may think about your trip to the beach with your family and then feel warm in your midsection. You may think about your horrible divorce and suddenly feel dizzy and exhausted. You might think about a task you need to accomplish and feel numb. As you read earlier, CBT attempts to change feelings by focusing on thoughts. This can sometimes be useful, but often we're well aware that our thoughts are illogical, yet we continue to spin.

The next time you feel overwhelmed, take a few minutes and notice your specific body sensations. Then get curious about what the sensations might be trying to communicate to you. *Then* ask yourself what you gain from staying stuck. Try not to allow judgment or shame to be part of this process. These exercises are about fact-finding and data-collecting. You do *not* need to toss another log onto the fire of self-blame, self-shame, and self-loathing. Journaling about body sensations and behavioral benefits can help speed relief up and slow symptoms down.

Conclusion

It is controversial to think about symptoms being responses from the body rather than mental illnesses, since it puts the full burden of responsibility on us to chart a course through our unexplored inner landscapes. Sometimes we settle on our diagnoses because it gives us connection and a sense of community with like-minded people. There is company in misery, and often as you get healthier and happier, you may find yourself quickly outgrowing the playgrounds and playmates from whom you derived comfort. As Marianne Williamson says in her book *A Return to Love*, "Our deepest fear is not that we are inadequate. Our deepest fear is that we are powerful beyond measure. It is our light, not our darkness, that most frightens us."

Emotions, feelings, and thoughts *all* need to be welcomed in the spirit of hospitality and curiosity. Areas of your life that you need to courageously explore include romantic relationships, friendships, work, family dynamics, spirituality, financial health, physical health, creativity, and playfulness. As you begin to accept your internal experiences, stuck no longer needs to play the role of benefactor. A willingness to experience your feelings, the gradual tolerance of uncomfortable body sensations, and the courage to examine what lies beneath the surface clear your paths to happiness and healing.

I don't enjoy feeling stuck. Even though I work with these practices day in and day out with other people, it is still challenging for me to do my personal work. Dealing with body sensations sometimes seems like another thing to add to our constantly bloated to-do lists. Often I hear clients say, "I don't know if I can do this, Britt—it's just so much work." True. Developing fluency in the language of sensation and learning to tap into the hidden benefits of stuck can be difficult—in the beginning. But no matter how frustrated I get with my body or my brain, my response to myself and to clients is always "Yes, this is hard. It takes work. But it takes more work to *not* do the work."

Relationships lost, job opportunities missed, days spent in bed, creative adventures ignored—to live in a perpetual state of stuck takes a ton of work. The myth is that there is an easy way. The truth is that there are only two ways—the hard way that goes around and around and around in circles, and the hard way that has a beginning, a middle, and an end.* The pain of facing feelings is often easier to navigate than the pain of avoiding them.

You can experience genuine joy only to the degree that you understand and accept all parts of yourself. The chapters that follow will help you learn to translate the language of your body. Unaddressed grief, unresolved anger, relational conflict, and unhealthy habits can all contribute to feeling stuck. You will learn how to decode your brain, develop boundary-setting strategies, and regain your ability to live an authentic life. When you understand the language of stuck, you can quickly find resources to reduce your symptoms and increase your happiness and well-being. Stuck is not something terrible happening to you. Stuck is a gift of the human design. It is created *by* you, *for* you, and *through* you.

---

*The change process has a beginning, a middle, and an end, but it is *not* a linear process.

Bottom-Line Takeaways

1. Most behaviors have perks—even "bad" behaviors.
2. There are many health benefits to staying stuck.
3. Understanding the function of your behavior is the key to changing it.
4. Staying stuck protects you from failure and rejection.
5. Your brain is wired for survival, not happiness.
6. Your nervous system is engineered to conserve energy.
7. Shame keeps you stuck.
8. Getting curious about your behaviors (without shaming yourself) gets you out of stuck.
9. Many of our symptoms are body responses and not mental illnesses.
10. It's usually harder to avoid your feelings than it is to feel your feelings.

Dos and Don'ts

Do	Don't
Connect with your physical body by saying to yourself, *Where in my body am I feeling things?*	Torture yourself with why questions. "Why am I being dramatic?" is *not* a helpful question.
Ask yourself what you gain from staying stuck.	Fool yourself into thinking that there are no benefits to staying stuck. There are *always* benefits to our behaviors, or the behaviors wouldn't be there.
Consider what could happen if you get out of stuck. Are there any relationships you are afraid will change as a result of your feeling better?	Feel shame about fearing change. Most people fear change to a degree.

Do	Don't
Remember that your brain does not always respond to logic, thoughts, or words.	Assume you are broken or crazy. There are always reasons for our behaviors—even if we don't know the reasons.

FIVE-MINUTE CHALLENGES

1. Write down all the critical and bullying things you've been saying to yourself and then add a compassionate rebuttal to each thing on the "bully" list. Here's an example:

Critical Self-Talk	Compassionate Self-Talk
"I'm so lazy. I suck."	"My brain thinks staying stuck will protect me from danger."
"I'm never going to be able to do things."	"I will do what I can and keep trying."

2. Get honest with yourself about the rewards of your behaviors. Do a cost-benefit analysis by copying the chart on the next page into a notebook.

COST-BENEFIT ANALYSIS

Behavior	Costs of Continuing the Behavior	Benefits of Continuing the Behavior	Benefits of Changing the Behavior

3. Fears/Needs/Resources list. Make a list of your three biggest fears, your three biggest needs, and the three biggest resources you have available to help you.

CHAPTER 3

The Myth of Motivation

You don't ask people with knives in their stomachs what would make them happy; happiness is no longer the point.

—Nick Hornby, *How to Be Good*

You were royally screwed if you were a woman during the 1500s.

The *Malleus Maleficarum* (translated as *The Hammer of Witches*) was the go-to manual for witch-hunting in the sixteenth century. *Malleus Maleficarum* may sound like a Hogwarts spell, but it was a highly regarded resource that fueled two centuries of witch-hunting mania in Europe. Reputable scholars and theologians wrote the text based on Exodus 22:18, which reads: "You shall not permit a sorceress to live." The *Malleus Maleficarum* represented the best thinking of its era, with severe and far-reaching consequences. The misogynistic and patriarchal view of witches and witchcraft continues to this day.

Or consider the medical treatment you'd receive during the 1500s. Isolation and beatings were the standard protocol to treat mental illness. People who suffered from psychological disorders were seen as either possessed by the devil or presenting a danger to society. To cure plague, doctors coated victims in mercury and placed them in the oven to ward off disease. Bloodletting (the practice of draining blood from the body) was standard operating procedure for fever. If you were under the care of Dr. François-Joseph-Victor Broussais, you'd end up covered in leeches. "[Dr. Broussais] was a great proponent of leech therapy along with aggressive bloodletting. He believed in placing leeches over the organ of the body deemed to be inflamed."* Yikes.

If you were fortunate enough to evade accusations of witchcraft and bites from bloodthirsty leeches, woe to those of the sixteenth century who desired cosmetic enhancement. Queen Elizabeth I was one of the earliest influencers. Her powdered face, neck ruffs, and elaborate jewelry were the envy of the time. Unfortunately, the makeup she reportedly favored—called Venetian ceruse—was a toxic mixture of water, lead, and vinegar. This concoction had horrific side effects like skin discoloration, loss of hair, and rotting teeth. Oh, the things we do for beauty. . . .

The best thinking of this time also produced a belief that persists to this day—the belief that feeling stuck is due to laziness or lack of motivation. The origin of the word *lazy* is attributed to sixteenth-century Middle Low German from the word *lasich*, meaning weak, feeble, and tired. Somehow, despite centuries of progress, laziness continues to be the shaming and judgmental explanation for science-based behavior. Beauty rituals thankfully evolved beyond Venetian ceruse. Medical treatment no longer defaults to bloodletting with leeches.† Pastors aren't allowed to kill their female-identifying congregants based upon the belief that "the manifest source of evil were in fact women, who seduced, charmed, and possessed men, often castrating them and keeping flocks of penises as amusing independent beings."‡ *Lazy* is a moral judgment—not a biological reality. The

> Lazy is a moral judgment—not a biological reality.

---

* *Bloodletting* refers to the practice of draining blood to cure disease. Gerry Greenstone, "The History of Bloodletting." *BC Medical Journal* 52, no. 1 (2010): 12–14. https://bcmj.org/premise/history-bloodletting.

† Technically bloodletting and leech therapy are still used, but they are not the go-to therapies for all our ailments.

‡ This quote comes from a fascinating article by Aleksandar Dimitrijevic, "Being Mad in Early Modern England." *Frontiers in Psychology* 6 (2015): 1740. doi: 10.3389/fpsyg.2015.01740.

word *lazy* in no way describes what actually happens in your brain when you find yourself glued to your couch.*

Brain Basics

By the end of this chapter, you'll replace the words *lazy* and *unmotivated* with practical information that you can use to get out of stuck. If your eyes are glazing over at the idea of reading an entire chapter about neurons and glial cells, have no fear. You don't need to know *all* the things—you just need to know enough to get yourself moving. Consider the following:

▸ You don't need to be an auto mechanic to drive your car. When you run out of gas, you know *enough* to get yourself to a gas station. You don't assume your car is hopelessly broken.

▸ You don't need to be a doctor to treat the symptoms of stomach flu. When you start feeling sick, you know *enough* to stay hydrated and rest. You don't think, *This is just who I am*.

▸ You don't need a degree in neuroscience to get unstuck. When you find yourself so amped up you can't focus or so exhausted you can't function, you just need to know *enough* about your brain to get to an effective solution.

We're also going to talk about trauma. Before you raise your hand and object, "But I don't have trauma," we're *not* going to discuss traumatic events like assault, abuse, or natural disasters. You won't be required to hunt for

---

*Reminder: The terms used here to describe the brain are incredibly simplified and intended to be metaphorical rather than literal descriptions.

memories or to get mad at your parents. If you don't identify as a trauma survivor, this chapter is for you.*

Why do we need to talk about trauma? When you want to be in *productive* mode but your brain is in *procrastination* mode, you're not lazy, you're experiencing a *trauma response*, otherwise known as survival brain.† Remember when you couldn't go anywhere or do anything in 2020? We all had to go into lockdown because the environment wasn't safe. Lockdown was due to a threat—it was *not* due to humanity's lack of motivation or inherent laziness. Survival brain puts you as well as all your objectives, plans, and ambitions into quarantine until it's convinced you are safe.

I'll explain.

Survival Brain Has Its Own Agenda

Your brain's primary function is to keep you alive, not to make you happy.

You may not *feel* like you need to conserve energy, but much of your brain's mechanisms are automatic—there's no ballot box where you get a vote in the process. Your brain wants to keep you safe from predators and keep you primed for action. Survival is everything. You may *want* to sit down and meditate, but your brain doesn't prioritize spiritual goals. You may *want* to finally start that course on entrepreneurship, but your brain doesn't prioritize career advancement.

Even if you're not in danger now, your brain may believe danger is coming later. Your brain's primary job is to anticipate your energy needs—a process called *allostasis*. In *Seven and a Half Lessons About the Brain*, Dr. Lisa

---

*If you're a survivor of sexual abuse, assault, violence, natural disasters, or a bad accident, you can still benefit from the information here.

†Technically survival brain could be called conservation brain, because the brain responds to opportunities and new information in addition to threats. Survival brain refers to the brain's response to *any* perceived energy need—not life-and-death threats exclusively.

Feldman Barrett writes: "Your brain's most important job is to control your body—to manage allostasis—by predicting energy needs before they arise so you can efficiently make worthwhile movements and survive." When your brain "budgets" energy inaccurately, you can spend too much energy or not generate enough energy. An inaccurate "brain budget" creates a mess of symptoms in your body and mind.

Think about this scenario: What if you believed the only way to light birthday candles was to use a blowtorch? The outcome would be a melted disaster and a likely visit from the fire department. A blowtorch provides *too much* energy for the task of candle-lighting. On the reverse end, imagine if you tried to warm up on a winter's day by standing near a lit match. You wouldn't get warm because a match doesn't provide *enough* energy for the task. When your brain uses more energy than normal or less energy than normal, this is called an *allostatic state*. Allostatic states are helpful if you're being chased by a bear or shooting for Olympic gold. They are *not* helpful if you want to relax after a long day of work or get started with a project. A *trauma response* is when your body goes into an allostatic state in the *absence* of a threat.[*]

Trauma Responses

Trauma responses can look like too *much* energy (anxiety/panic/ADD) or too *little* energy (depression/fatigue/procrastination). Getting out of stuck requires a basic understanding of trauma—even if you don't think you have it.

"Why is my brain worried about danger when I'm totally safe?"

Your *mind* may think you're safe, but it's your *body* that calls the plays. You do *not* get to consciously decide whether your body should feel safe or unsafe.

---

[*] "Allostatic states can produce wear and tear on the regulatory systems in the brain and body. The terms 'allostatic load' and 'allostatic overload' refer to the cumulative results of an allostatic state." Bruce S. McEwen, "Stressed or Stressed Out: What Is the Difference?" *Journal of Psychiatry & Neuroscience* 30, no. 5 (2005): 315–18. https://www.ncbi.nlm.nih.gov/pmc/articles/PMC1197275/.

In *The Pocket Guide to the Polyvagal Theory*, Dr. Stephen W. Porges writes: "Perhaps our misunderstanding of the role of safety is based on an assumption that we think we know what safety means. This assumption needs to be challenged, because there may be an inconsistency between the words we use to describe safety and our bodily feelings of safety." Most of us are never taught to describe our internal cues for safety and danger. For example, when was the last time you asked yourself, *Where in my body am I feeling a sense of safety right now?* Genetics, medical history, family of origin, environment, relational circumstances, and even the weather can impact your unconscious perception of safety. Dr. Porges adds: "Outside the realm of conscious awareness, our nervous system is continuously evaluating risk in the environment, making judgments, and setting priorities for behaviors that are adaptive."

Logic and reason are not part of the safety-planning process. Laziness and lack of motivation are not bad habits—they are *trauma responses*. Addiction expert Dr. Gabor Maté writes: "We no longer sense what is happening in our bodies and cannot therefore act in self-preserving ways. The physiology of stress eats away at our bodies . . . because we no longer have the competence to recognize its signals." When you don't know you have trauma, it is impossible to move past it. If you're not convinced that you have trauma, consider the indicators in the following list.

SIGNS OF UNRESOLVED TRAUMA

- Indecisiveness
- Over-apologizing
- Difficulty saying no
- ADD/ADHD/OCD*
- People-pleasing
- Perfectionism

---

*ADD/ADHD/OCD are often trauma responses, but that does *not* mean you can't use medication to manage the symptoms. Always speak with your doctor before going off any medications.

- ▸ Mind racing
- ▸ Difficulty relaxing
- ▸ Hating surprises
- ▸ Procrastinating
- ▸ Feeling lazy when you want to be productive
- ▸ Inability to stop working when you want to rest
- ▸ Exaggerated startle response (always jumpy)
- ▸ Difficulty enjoying sex
- ▸ Difficulty enjoying food without guilt

"But wait," you may protest, "I was never in a war, assaulted, in a natural disaster, or anything like that! How can you say that I have trauma?"

"Having trauma" does *not* mean that you had a bad childhood. It does *not* mean you repressed a horrible memory. It does *not* mean that you were abused. Why is there so much confusion about trauma? Here's a fact that might surprise you:

Therapists *aren't* required to learn about the brain *or* about trauma.

Unless therapists sign up for many extra years of specialized training, we aren't taught about the brain,* and we're not required to know how to identify and treat trauma.† Many of my clients report that they can't sleep, can't relax, can't achieve their goals, and can't manage their thoughts. Because they never learned what it means to "have trauma," I often hear things like:

- ▸ "But I don't have trauma—I always had enough money, enough to eat, and a safe place to live."

---

*On the occasions when therapists are provided with education about the brain, it's often outdated.

†Therapists are not required to know about trauma, and many of them do *not* disclose their training limitations. Make sure to ask your therapist if they have trauma training. If they don't, be *very* careful about accepting their diagnosis as gospel truth.

- ▸ "But I don't have trauma—I wasn't abused as a child."
- ▸ "But I don't have trauma—nothing bad ever happened to me."
- ▸ "But I don't have trauma—my family is awesome."
- ▸ "Trauma? Never heard of her . . ."

If we go back to our earlier example, if you don't know to fill up your gas tank, your car stays parked. If you don't know to rest during the stomach flu, your body stays sick. If you don't know how trauma works, you'll stay stuck. So let's put this out there in the simplest possible language:

> You have unresolved trauma. So do I. So does everyone. As long as you're human, you are going to have trauma to a degree.

This statement tends to aggravate people. As a survivor of domestic violence and sexual abuse, I get it. Some survivors balk at the idea that everyone has trauma. They say, "Well, if everyone has it, then no one has it. If we all have trauma, doesn't that minimize what happened to *me*?" Conversely, people who *don't* identify as survivors also stiffen at the notion of trauma. Their concerns sound like: "Well, if I have trauma, does this then mean that I have to hate my parents, quit my job, and spend the next decade in therapy?" We need to put this debate to rest. In order to figure out if you have trauma, it helps to start with a definition.

What *Is* Trauma?

The definition I use as a trauma clinician comes from Dr. Peter Levine, the developer of Somatic Experiencing, a body-oriented approach to trauma healing. Dr. Levine's bio states that his work is the result of a "multidisciplinary study of stress physiology, psychology, ethology, biology, neuroscience, indigenous healing practices, and medical biophysics." He defines trauma as anything that is "too much, too fast, or too soon." Trauma is an *in-*

ternal process—not an *external* event. Dr. Levine writes: "Trauma is not what happens to us, but what we hold inside in the absence of an empathic witness." Trauma is your brain's inability to process and metabolize information. In simpler terms, trauma is *brain indigestion.** A trauma response is what happens as a result of brain indigestion. Though the word *trauma* sounds scary, it is simply a clinical way of saying your brain is overwhelmed.

You may not identify as a trauma survivor, but have you ever felt overwhelmed?

Have you ever felt like you were stuck in the off position? Have you ever felt baffled because no matter how much you yelled at yourself, you still couldn't manage to get started on your to-do list?

That's a trauma response. Your brain decided the best way to survive was to shut down.

Have you ever felt like you couldn't sleep, couldn't relax, couldn't slow down and focus, or couldn't stop feeling the pressure to perform perfectly?

That's also a trauma response. This is often referred to as fight-or-flight mode.

Myths About Trauma

Often the very things we think make us broken are our brains doing exactly what they're supposed to do to keep us alive. Trauma responses are often misdiagnosed and mislabeled as mental illness.[†] Mental *issues* are not necessarily mental *illnesses*. Symptoms are creative manifestations of unmet needs.[‡] Trauma is not an illness—it is

> Trauma is not an illness—it is an injury and it can heal.

---

* Metaphor alert. *Brain indigestion* is not a medical term or a literal description of your anatomy.

† Trauma responses do not negate the reality of mental illness, debilitating symptoms, or the need for medication.

‡ Healing from trauma requires the presence of choices. Some people have no choices about finances, oppression, systemic brokenness, or safety. We perpetuate trauma when we place the burden of healing on those for whom no healing resources are accessible.

an injury and it can heal. The following chart illustrates the main myths about trauma.

Trauma Myth	Trauma Truth
You need to forgive or you won't heal.	Forgiveness is a spiritual ideal. It is not required to heal trauma.
Procrastination is a character weakness.	Procrastination is a trauma response in your brain.
Laziness is why you can't get things done.	Laziness is also a trauma response.
If they didn't mean to hurt me, it shouldn't bother me.	Intention does not negate impact. I may not have intended to hit you with my car, but my good intentions do not unbreak your legs.
You can think your way out of procrastination.	Positive affirmations are great once logic is readily available. Until your brain perceives safety, thoughts won't work.* *"When the alarm bell of the emotional brain keeps signaling that you are in danger, no amount of insight will silence it." Bessel van der Kolk, *The Body Keeps the Score: Brain, Mind, and Body in the Healing of Trauma.*
You can shame your way out of laziness.	If yelling at yourself was effective, you'd be good to go.
It takes a lifetime to heal.	You do not need to spend ten years in therapy to get your brain out of survival mode.
If I can't remember something, it can't have an impact on me.	Your body records all your experiences—even the ones your mind forgets.
You need to relive your memories in order to heal them.	You do not need to dig for memories to get unstuck.
Trauma is a mental illness.	Trauma is an injury. It can heal.
Only the things that happen to *you* can cause trauma.	You can be traumatized by witnessing someone else's experience. This is called secondary trauma.

Trauma Myth	Trauma Truth
You need to know why you feel what you feel. If you don't, it means there's something wrong with you.	You may not understand why things bother you or trigger you, but everything makes sense in context. You are *not* crazy.
You just need to relax and take a breath.	Trying to force relaxation with deep breaths can retraumatize your body and make things worse.
Trauma is caused only by bad things.	Trauma can be caused by *anything* that exceeds your brain's capacity to process.
You need to tell your story to heal.	You do not need to tell your story—or to even *know* your story—in order to heal.

At this point people tend to scratch their heads and wonder, "Wait . . . if trauma is not what happens *to* us but what happens *inside* us, then what do you call abuse, oppression, war, and so forth?" We need to differentiate between trauma, traumatic events, trauma-inducing events, and trauma responses:

▸ **Trauma:** An *internal* state in which your brain is unable to digest or process information. Another way to say this is overwhelm.

▸ **Traumatic Event:** Events everyone agrees are horrific, with the potential to have lasting consequences—abuse, war, natural disaster, systemic oppression, racism, poverty, sexual assault, violence.

▸ **Trauma-Inducing Event:** Events you don't think of as traumatic or bad but which can still cause distressing symptoms—giving birth, getting married, undergoing surgery, moving to a new city, losing weight, dating, starting a new job.

▸ **Trauma Response:** This happens when your brain *perceives* an energy need and either floods your body with "get-up-and-go juice" (panic/anxiety/ADD) or shuts your system down (depression/fatigue/procrastination). A trauma response is based on your brain's *perception*—it does not matter whether the need is real.

Common Objections to the Trauma Explanation

"You're claiming the reason I don't feel like cleaning the house is because of a trauma response? That sounds like an excuse to me."

If you're stuck on hour five of a Twitter scroll-a-thon, it's not because you lack motivation—it's because your brain thinks you need to conserve energy. The word *motivate* is as problematic to the healing process as the word *lazy*. The term *motivation* is derived from the Latin word *movere*, meaning to move. Motivation is defined as a goal-directed and conscious process. It is a *voluntary* effort. But many of your body's responses are *involuntary*. It makes absolutely no sense to condemn yourself for an automatic body response. Dr. Peter Levine writes: "Animals do not view freezing as a sign of inadequacy or weakness, nor should we."

"Does this mean I get to tell my boss, 'I really wanted to come to work today, but my survival brain made me watch cat videos on TikTok'?"

No. Understanding the physiology of survival brain does not excuse procrastination—it *explains* it. If you don't know what's happening in your brain, there is no way to identify an effective solution. Calling yourself lazy doesn't create change—it creates *shame*. Knowing there is a science-based explanation doesn't mean it's okay to stay on the couch. It means you now have the information needed to get *off* the couch. We'll discuss ways to coax your brain out of survival mode later in this chapter. For the time being, all you need to remember is this: if shaming yourself into healthy behavior worked, it would have worked by now.

"I have so much trouble staying focused. It's like there's a million things going on in my head and I can't even manage the simplest of tasks. It takes me two hours to send a three-sentence email!"

I hear you. If you struggle to focus—if simple tasks feel like giant mountains—this is not because you're broken. A brain that feels threatened is not going to be able to focus on anything except survival. Imagine trying to remember your to-do list while a giant tiger is about to eat you.

"You're telling me that I have trauma. But if nothing bad ever happened to me, why do I have it?"

Think about the food you eat. *Anything* can cause indigestion. You know if you ingest contaminated food, it's likely that you'll get sick. But you can also experience indigestion from the same meal that you've eaten a million times. Not all foods are going to cause indigestion. But all foods have the *potential* to cause indigestion. Trauma is the same. If you experience war, abuse, natural disaster, or assault, the likelihood that you'll have symptoms is high.* But normal things can cause trauma too. Your brain is a highly complex network. Your body receives infinite pieces of information every second of every minute of every day. Not everything is going to overwhelm your brain. But everything has the *potential* to overwhelm your brain. The reality of indigestion doesn't stop me from enjoying cheesecake. The reality of trauma doesn't need to stop you from enjoying life.

"I know things weren't perfect—everyone has ups and downs. But I firmly believe you need to leave the past in the past and move on. I believe you shouldn't sweat the small stuff."

Your brain has its own definition of what constitutes the small stuff. If your brain thinks you're in danger, seemingly small stuff becomes big stuff. If it was truly possible to keep the past in the past, no one would get stuck. A system that knows the past is in the past will *not* manifest symptoms. The past stays present until it's processed. The goal is to metabolize our experiences—not to get over them. Metabolizing your experiences means you can feel your feelings without overwhelm—that is, you can remember painful memories without cringing and you mostly feel at home in your body.

> The past stays present until it's processed.

---

*Not every traumatic event will cause a trauma response.

The Truth About Laziness and Motivation

There is no such thing as an unmotivated or a lazy person. Humans are *always* motivated. Your brain is motivated either to make conscious choices or to survive threats.* When you say, "I struggle with motivation," what you *really* mean is "My brain thinks it needs to conserve energy to keep me alive." When I hear clients describe themselves as "unable to focus," what they often mean is "My brain thinks I need to keep moving so I don't get eaten by a cheetah."

Survival responses are based on a wide variety of factors, including genetics, biology, access to safety and resources, privilege, family support, social networks, community engagement, and medical history. Fortunately, it is not necessary to know *why* your brain created a trauma response or to *what* stimuli your brain was reacting. Logically you may think everything is fine, but if your brain perceives a threat, survival physiology wins every time. Sometimes the perception of danger results in down feelings—fatigue, depression, lack of motivation. Other times the perception of danger results in up feelings—stress, panic, anxiety, and distraction.

The Myth of Balance

Part of the reason you sometimes feel crazy is because you've likely been taught to seek balance in your life. Many wellness and health gurus teach us to seek balance. There's definitely a place for balance-seeking, particularly in our secret world of thoughts. (We'll cover this in the next chapter.) But balance is not how a healthy nervous system operates. In fact, true balance is physically impossible—your body can't be ready to dance and also be ready to

---

* "The reflective brain response that spurs motivation cannot take place during high-stress emotional states." Chelsea Mize, "The Neuroscience of Motivation and How to Increase Motivation." Helping People Connect, September 6, 2021. https://www.pgi.com/blog/2017/08/neuroscience-motivation-increase-motivation/.

sleep at the same time. Balance is not the goal. Rather than a static (fixed) nervous system, a dynamic (mobile) system is the goal. A dynamic system is capable of change and smoothly transitions between active and resting states.

A Healthy Nervous System Is *Dynamic*

What It's SUPPOSED to Look Like:
Dynamic

Rest / Activity
Peaceful / Excited
Calm / Energized
Self-Care / Care of Others
Relaxation / Productivity

Your autonomic nervous system* includes two divisions: on (sympathetic nervous system/SNS) and off (parasympathetic nervous system/PNS). Think of the SNS as your gas pedal and the PNS as your brake pedal. When you're driving a car, you can smoothly transition between pedals. There's no lurching, screeching brakes, or squealing tires. A healthy nervous system will smoothly alternate between up and down.

Stuck in *Up Mode*

Sometimes your nervous system switches into up mode. This is called a *sympathetic response*. When your nervous system shifts into up mode, you'll

---

*There's a third component to your autonomic nervous system called the enteric nervous system, but that goes beyond the scope of this chapter. The main things to know about the enteric nervous system are: (1) It's located in your gut. (2) Gut health is key to mental health. (3) If you're not pooping regularly and properly, your moods can be *severely* impacted.

experience distraction, restlessness, inability to relax, anxiety, panic, and irritability. During a sympathetic response, your blood pressure goes up, your heart rate increases, your digestion goes off-line, and your body is primed either to fight for its life or to flee the scene. Sympathetic responses are incredibly useful during emergencies. But a nervous system stuck on up is like driving a car without brakes. An *overactive sympathetic response* is when your body picks up danger cues when none are present. The abundance of stress hormones released during an overactive sympathetic response can create panic, inexplicable anger outbursts, emotional overload, insomnia, racing thoughts, inflammation, breathing problems, and profuse sweating.*

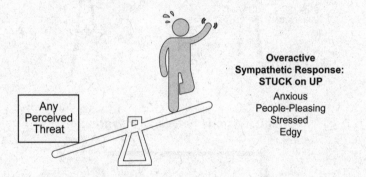

Any Perceived Threat

Overactive Sympathetic Response: STUCK on UP
Anxious
People-Pleasing
Stressed
Edgy

Stuck in *Down Mode*—Your Braking System

Your parasympathetic nervous system is your braking system, or down mode. You need your regular brakes to slow down, but you need your emergency brake *only* when you want to immobilize the car. If your emergency brake is engaged, you're not going anywhere, no matter how many affirmations you chant. Just as your car has regular brakes and an emergency brake, your PNS has a regular braking system and an emergency braking system.

When you feel rested, calm, and peaceful, your regular brakes are engaged.

---

* If you're experiencing medical symptoms, put down this book and see a medical doctor (MD). Always rule out medical causes with an MD before taking a psychological approach to healing.

This is also known as a *low tone dorsal* vagal state*. If your emergency brake kicks on, you'll feel exhausted, immobilized, depressed, frozen, and numb.†
The emergency brake is called a *high tone dorsal vagal state*. When you feel energized, socially connected, and curious, that's called a *ventral vagal state*.

Okay, enough terminology. The academic world is fond of using big

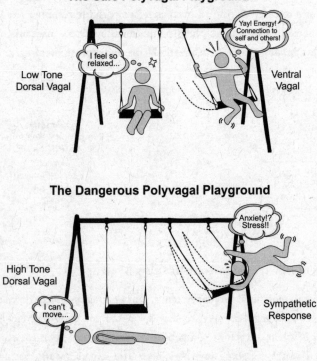

---

words (and lots of them) to describe things. The image of a swing set provides a much easier way to think about the nervous system.

Okay, so I Have Trauma—Now What?

The best way to manage a trauma response is to develop fluency in the language of *body sensations*. Most people are not taught to recognize bodily feelings of danger and safety, and most therapists aren't trained to ask. Mental health is not about strength versus weakness. It's about the perception of *safety* versus the perception of *danger*. A brain that feels safe has no need to produce symptoms. The next section provides exercises to help your body find its way to safety. None of the suggestions here are intended to be magical cures or to replace therapy or medical care. It is also important to remember that if your environment is not safe, your survival brain is going to stay activated. This is *not* your fault.

Stuck on On—How to Manage a Sympathetic Response

1. Say to yourself, *I am having a trauma response. This is a physiological process. I'm not crazy.*
2. Make a list of people, places, and things that you love. Notice how your body feels as you think about hugging your best friend, sitting on a beach, or curling up with your favorite book.
3. Use your senses. Weighted blankets, essential oils, soft music, and warm tea can all help your "seesaw" come back down.
4. Count backward from the number 31.*

---

*Why 31? It's a weird number that will immediately help to jolt your brain back into thinking mode. Any number that you wouldn't normally think to use will do the trick. This is an anecdotal intervention.

5. Notice *five* things you can see, *four* things you can hear, *three* things you can touch, *two* things you can smell, and *one* thing you can taste.

6. Push as hard as you can against a door or a wall. Notice your muscles firing. Step back, take a break, repeat three times.

7. Do simple math problems in your head. You can keep elementary school math flash cards on hand to help alleviate a panic response. Simple thinking tasks will help your brain reorient itself.

8. *Name* the sensations inside your body. Say to yourself out loud, *I feel tension in my neck. I feel tightness in my stomach. I feel heat in my face.* Then look for *one* place in your body where you feel neutral or calm. (Most people can access neutral by noticing random areas like their left kneecap or their right ring finger.) Focus your attention first on the neutral area, then on the tense area, then on the neutral area. Do this for four minutes.

9. *Don't* ask why you feel panic. *Do* ask who or what will help you feel safe.

10. If you have a dog or a cat, gently put your hand on their heart and count their heartbeats for three minutes.

Stuck on Off—How to Manage a High Tone Dorsal Vagal State

1. Remind yourself you are not lazy or unmotivated. Tell yourself, *I am having a trauma response. This is a thing. I am not crazy.*

2. Get cold. Splash ice-cold water on your face, hold ice cubes in your hand, put an ice pack on your neck, or jump into the coldest possible shower you can stand.

3. Hum or sing. There's a reason people have chanted *Om* since the sixth century.*

---

* "A sensation of vibration is experienced during audible 'OM' chanting. This has the potential

4. Social connection is powerful medicine. Connect with a human over the phone (good), over video chat (better), or in person (best).*

5. *Don't* ask *why* you're feeling frozen. *Do* ask who or what might help you feel safer.

6. *Don't* use hyperbolic (exaggerated) language like "I feel *buried*" or "I'm *drowning*." This language reinforces the stress response. Instead, get *really* specific: "I need to call my son's teacher, pick up my prescription, and finish a proposal for work." Write down the specific tasks. This will help your brain click back into solution mode.

7. Suck on a lemon.† This sounds weird. But it can help shock your brain out of shutdown mode.

8. Open and close your mouth, then move your head. Then stretch your arms and legs. This will help cue your brain that there is not a wildebeest sitting on your chest.

9. Grab both ends of a blanket and wring it out as you would if it was soaking wet. Notice your muscles firing as you do this. Take a break, repeat three times.

10. If you have a safe and willing friend or partner, make eye contact with them for two to three minutes. It's super-awkward, but you'll get a bonus dose of energy if you both end up laughing.

---

for vagus nerve stimulation through its auricular branches and the effects on the brain thereof." Bangalore G. Kalyani, Ganesan Venkatasubramanian, Rashmi Arasappa, et al., "Neurohemody-namic Correlates of 'OM' Chanting: A Pilot Functional Magnetic Resonance Imaging Study." *International Journal of Yoga* 4, no. 1: 3–6. https://www.ncbi.nlm.nih.gov/pmc/articles/PMC3099099/.

* "You can use the social nervous system to identify that you are safe. You can look around and listen for cues of safety or engage in strategies such as calm, slow breathing to help you relax. All of these actions use the action systems above the diaphragm." Arielle Schwartz, "Polyvagal Theory Helps Unlock Symptoms of PTSD." https://drarielleschwartz.com/polyvagal-theory -unlocks-symptoms-of-ptsd-dr-arielle-schwartz/#.YEzaaV1KifQ.

† This intervention is anecdotal, not evidence-based.

Your Brain Isn't Finished Yet

Life in the modern world is complicated, but it's preferable to the witch-hunts and "lunatic asylums" of the past. In *The Devil's Doctor*, Philip Ball writes, "No matter who you were in sixteenth-century Europe, you could be sure of two things: you would be lucky to reach fifty years of age, and you could expect a life of discomfort and pain." Medical discoveries about noninvasive surgery and antibiotics allow you to enjoy a longer and more comfortable life. Psychological discoveries about trauma and the brain allow you to enjoy a *happier* and more *creative* life. Dr. Daniel J. Siegel, clinical professor of psychiatry at the UCLA School of Medicine, writes: "We are always in a perpetual state of being created and creating ourselves." This perpetual state of change and growth is called neuroplasticity.

Neuroplasticity means your brain is a work in progress—*not* a finished product. Even your most frustrating habits are not set in stone. The brain you have now isn't the brain you'll have a week, a month, or a year from now. The degree to which you have choices is the degree to which you can heal. In the novel *Wicked*, author Gregory Maguire writes: "Remember this: Nothing is written in the stars. Not these stars, nor any others. No one controls your destiny." You can't change anything about the past. But you can change *everything* about your future when you understand how your brain processes the *present*.

You are *not* lazy, crazy, or unmotivated.

BOTTOM-LINE TAKEAWAYS

1. Trauma is brain indigestion. We all experience it to one degree or another.
2. A trauma response is the result of your brain miscalculating your body's energy needs.

3. When your nervous system gets stuck on up, you feel panicked/anxious/distracted.
4. When your nervous system gets stuck on down, you feel tired/depressed/frozen.
5. Your unconscious brain gets to decide whether you are safe.
6. "Lazy" is a moral judgment—not a biological reality.
7. Your brain is always motivated. It's motivated either to make choices or to survive threats.
8. You don't need a balanced system—you need a dynamic (mobile) system.
9. Trauma *explains* behavior—it does not *excuse* behavior.
10. Trauma is not an illness. It is an injury—and it can heal.

Dos and Don'ts

Do	Don't
Remind yourself that even if you don't know why you feel unmotivated or lazy, that doesn't mean your brain isn't *unconsciously* sensing danger.	Tell yourself you are freaking out for no reason. There's always a reason—even if you don't know what it is.
Encourage yourself when you feel stuck. Remind yourself that your brain is trying to help you, not to hurt you.	Call yourself lazy or unmotivated. Survival/conservation physiology is *unconscious* and *automatic*.
Use sensory interventions (touch/taste/sight/sound/smell) when you're stuck on up or down.	Try to think your way out of a trauma response. You can't think or talk your way out of automatic physiological processes.
Ask yourself what might help you feel safer or less threatened in this moment.	Assume there's something wrong with you. Your brain is doing exactly what your brain is designed to do.

FIVE-MINUTE CHALLENGES

1. A powerful antidote to a trauma response is *making a choice*. Think of ten small choices you can make in the next five minutes. This can be as simple as what to wear, what to eat, what music to put on, or on what piece of furniture you want to sit.

2. Turn an overwhelming response into digestible pieces of information. Naming issues in as detailed a way as possible can often help your brain to stay in solution mode and out of survival mode. For example, instead of thinking, *I'm drowning*, write down the specifics of your situation on paper: *I have to switch the kids' weekend with their father. I have until Tuesday to finish my work project. I need to pay the overdue water bill. I have to get to the dentist to fix a cavity.*

3. Create a Mary Poppins–esque wellness tote. Put things you can smell, touch, look at, and taste in a bag or box. (This is also a great exercise to do with kids.) You can include coloring books and markers, sour candies, squishy balls, essential oil rollers, fidget toys, pictures of your pets, and notes reminding yourself that trauma responses *are* a thing and you are *not* crazy.

CHAPTER 4

Shadow Intelligence

Why You Need the Parts of Yourself You Hate

"Everyone knows you cannot sweep away shadows," said Skunk.
"You can't hide from them or run away from them either,"
said Rabbit.

—Ann Tompert, *Nothing Sticks Like a Shadow*

I remember the final time I smoked crystal meth.

For months I had been telling myself I didn't really have a problem. After all, if I don't actually buy or prep the drugs myself, surely that doesn't count? It was easy to stay in denial—up until this point I had always used hard drugs in the company of other people. I repeatedly told myself I was merely a social user, not an addict. But this time was different—I was all alone in a dirty bathroom at five in the morning. The fragments of my remaining ego burned along with the crystal shards in the glass pipe. As the white smoke swirled through the long tube, I thought to myself, *I think I have a problem.*

That was the moment I met my shadow.

What Is "The Shadow"?

"The Shadow" sounds like a Halloween movie or an R. L. Stine book, but don't worry—it isn't anything scary or mystical. In nature, physical shadows are created when light is blocked. Psychological shadows are created when *awareness* is blocked. "The Shadow" is a metaphor used to describe any parts of ourselves we are ashamed to admit or afraid to encounter. Some people have a creativity shadow—they think they should always be *practical*. Others have an anger shadow—they think they should always be *nice*. You might be so worried about people thinking you're selfish that you neglect your own needs and desires. Or maybe you hide your talents because you feel afraid of judgment and criticism.

In the book *Shadow Life*, author Oli Anderson writes: "Your Shadow is all of the things, 'positive' and 'negative,' that you've denied about yourself and hidden beneath the surface of the mask you forgot that you're wearing." *Shadow work*—which is just a fancy way to say "being honest *with* yourself *about* yourself"—is the focus of this chapter. When you identify, understand, and befriend your shadows, they no longer have power over your actions. Swiss psychiatrist Carl Jung wrote extensively about shadows. He said, "Until you make the unconscious conscious, it will direct your life and you will call it fate."

Why You Need Your Shadow

Jung also wrote: "How can I be substantial if I do not cast a shadow? I must have a dark side also if I am to be whole." Wholehearted living requires *wholeness*. But most of us aren't taught how to be whole. Instead, we're taught to split off from any thoughts, feelings, or qualities that aren't socially acceptable. Children learn from an early age to divide the world into "good guys" and "bad guys." We're trained to value goodness over wholeness. Jenna Maclaine writes: "But, truly, the darkness is simply a piece of the whole, neither good nor evil unless you make it so." Your shadow is similar to a fire—fire has the potential to provide heat and comfort *and* it has the potential to cause pain and destruction. Your shadow is neither good nor bad until you act. Take the examples of Bruce Wayne in *Batman Begins* and Walter White in *Breaking Bad*:

> We're trained to value goodness over wholeness.

Bruce Wayne: The pain from his parents' murder creates a deep well of rage. His mentor warns him: "Your anger gives you great power, but if you let it, it will destroy you."* Instead of denying or suppressing his feelings, Bruce chooses to create an alter ego (Batman) through which to channel his anger toward injustice. In *Batman Begins*, Bruce Wayne says, "It's not who I am underneath . . . but what I *do* that defines me." Bruce Wayne/Batman is an example of *shadow integration*—bringing your dark side into awareness. He's conscious of his shadow—but not ruled by it.

Walter White: In contrast to Bruce Wayne's successful shadow integration, Walter White in *Breaking Bad* demonstrates the flip side—shadow splitting. Walter White was the epitome of a "nice" guy—a gentle, timid, soft-spoken chemistry teacher. But after his cancer diagnosis, he is overtaken by his shadows. Eventually he transforms into a vicious drug kingpin. Power and corruption gradually erode all traces of the "good" guy known as Walter White—he even changes his name to Heisenberg.†

Bruce Wayne and Walter White are extreme examples. But even if you don't drive a Batmobile or manufacture meth, we *all* have parts of ourselves

---

* This quote was delivered by Liam Neeson's character Ducard in *Batman Begins*. As it turns out (spoiler alert), Ducard had a *major* shadow—he turns out to be the villainous Ra's al Ghul (Head of the Demon).

† Fun fact: Heisenberg's uncertainty principle says: "the act of measurement will itself interfere with the system being measured in unpredictable ways." https://dictionary.apa.org/uncertainty-principle.

that we hide from ourselves. A less intense illustration of shadow work can be seen in *The Devil Wears Prada*.

> ***The Devil Wears Prada***: Protagonist Andy Sachs is an aspiring (and sartorially challenged) writer who judges and criticizes the fashionistas with whom she works—particularly her ruthless and cutthroat boss, Miranda Priestly. Andy is so unaware of her shadows that she gradually sacrifices her personal and professional relationships. She trades authenticity for job security (and a pile of designer clothes). By the end of the movie, Andy is horrified to discover that she isn't *better* than her boss—she's exactly the same. Once she confronts her shadows, she is free to make conscious choices. Andy decides to leave the fashion world to pursue a job she loves.*

Everyone carries the full spectrum of human potential—the good, the bad, and the WTF. Those weird, random thoughts you sometimes think? I have them too. Margaret Atwood wrote: "If we were all on trial for our thoughts, we would all be hanged." I was so desperate to hide from my thoughts that I was willing to trade my sanity, safety, and integrity to do it.

The problem with trying to hide from our shadows? It doesn't work.

Increasing Your Shadow Intelligence (SQ)

My friend Kristen Asher-Kirk says, "When we accept ourselves entirely, we have more energy to give ourselves and to the people we love." It takes enormous effort to keep the things you know out of sight and out of mind. Think of holding a beach ball under the water. This is energy that you *could* use to

---

* Interesting side note: At the end of the movie, we see Andy happily working at her new job, but in contrast to her earlier fashion flubs she is now dressed in a stylish outfit. This is the perfect demonstration of shadow integration. Andy is *aware* of her desire to be fashionable, but she is no longer *ruled* by it.

pursue your dreams, enjoy your family, or invest in your business. Any qualities we hide in the shadows tend to show up sideways in our lives as mental health symptoms, relational difficulties, or inexplicable triggers. Whenever your actions diverge from your authenticity, your shadow grows in power. French philosopher Gilles Deleuze writes: "The shadow escapes from the body like an animal we had been sheltering." The proverbial midlife crisis is a classic example of this phenomenon. When you have a low quotient of shadow awareness, internal pressure builds and eventually erupts.

You've likely heard of IQ (intelligence quotient) and EQ (emotional intelligence), but to get unstuck you also need to have what I've termed SQ, or shadow intelligence. People high in SQ know their shadows inside and out. They are free to pursue their dreams instead of doing what Gay Hendricks calls "upper-limiting"—the unconscious tendency to sabotage when we get close to achieving our goals.[*] The higher your SQ, the more capacity you have to accept your imperfections *and* to enjoy your successes. Daniel Goleman, author of *Emotional Intelligence*, provides this equation:

$$IQ \text{ (intelligence quotient)} + EQ \text{ (emotional intelligence)} = success$$

Goleman's equation is powerful and largely accurate. However, plenty of people achieve success but *still* feel a nagging emptiness. Success without wholeness feels lonely and unsatisfying. The piece that's missing? Shadow intelligence. When you add shadow intelligence to the equation, suddenly you have a powerful formula for getting unstuck:

$$IQ + EQ + SQ \text{ (shadow intelligence)} = success \text{ and the freedom to enjoy it}$$

Another benefit of shadow work? When you stop avoiding yourself, you can access hidden gems inside your shadow like creativity, energy, and grit. In Pixar's *Inside Out*, the character Joy thinks Sadness is dangerous and

---

[*] The concept of upper-limiting comes from Gay Hendricks's *The Big Leap*.

destructive. Joy scrambles to keep Sadness away from everyone and every-thing. But in the end, Joy learns the value of *all* feelings—and ultimately it is Sadness who saves the day.

Even though Sadness is essential to our well-being (as the character proved in the plot of *Inside Out*), many of us continue to suppress painful thoughts and feelings. But it's only when you're willing to explore the caves of discomfort that you can access your shadow's healing properties. Shadow experts Dr. Connie Zweig and Dr. Steve Wolf write: "As each layer of shadow is mined from the darkness, as each fear is faced . . . the gold shines through."

Shadow Quality	Potential Gift
Resentment	Shows you where you need boundaries
Procrastination	Helps to protect you from potential threat
Envy	Points you toward your desires
Gossip	Uncovers your need for connection
Guilt	Proves you aren't a sociopath

Every shadow part has the potential to provide valuable gifts.

What Are Shadow "Parts"?

We've all had a similar experience. Part of you knows that you should eat vegetables and exercise, but there's this other part that seems to take over and then you end up eating a pint of Chunky Monkey while watching an entire season of *Law & Order: SVU* until three A.M.

That other part of you? That's a shadow part.

Like it or not, you have nice parts *and* mean parts. Go-getter parts *and* procrastinator parts. Parts who feel empathy *and* parts who judge. You're not a hypocrite and you're not crazy—you simply live in a physical and psychological world of opposites. Up and down. Night and day. Joy and sorrow.

Sickness and health. In *31 Ways to Happiness*, Awdhesh Singh writes: "Your happiness depends on your ability to balance the opposites rather than sticking to only one of the truths while ignoring all others. When you avoid something for long, over a period of time, it creates a craving in you that can disturb the peace of your mind and make you suffer immensely."

> *"Okay, Britt, so are you saying I now have permission to let my shadow parts come out and do whatever they feel like doing?"*

No.

The solution is neither to ignore your shadow parts nor to permit them to run wild. The solution is to develop a relationship* with and an outlet for your shadow parts—we'll talk about how to do this in the next section. When you begin to get curious about your inner world, you realize it's often the parts of yourself you hate the most that are trying the hardest to help you.†

We All Have Multiple Personalities

When I first introduce the idea of different parts to clients, almost everyone immediately panics and asks, "Are you saying that I have multiple personality disorder?"

No.

Having multiple personalities is *not* the same as having multiple personality disorder.‡ Every complex system contains multiple parts. Earth is a

---

* In *A Little Book on the Human Shadow*, Robert Bly wrote: "every part of our personality that we do not love will become hostile to us."

† Shadow work and parts language can help *explain* behavior—but nothing *excuses* behavior. "My shadow made me do it" is not a valid excuse.

‡ Multiple personality disorder (MPD) is no longer a diagnosis. It is now called dissociative

single planet, but within the planet are multiple landmasses, bodies of water, animals, and weather patterns. A tree is a single organism comprising multiple branches, bark, leaves, and a root system. Your physical body houses multiple organs, joints, and muscles. Your psyche is no different. It is a complex system made up of multiple subparts or sub-personalities. Intuitively, most people are aware of their multiplicity. Walt Whitman put it this way: "I am large, I contain multitudes." Think of the language you hear daily:

> ▸ "I know there is nothing to worry about—but part of me is freaking out anyway."
> ▸ "It would be really good for me to take breaks from work—but part of me won't let me slow down."
> ▸ "I love my family—but part of me sometimes feels resentful."
> ▸ "I really want to get this business going—but there's this part of me who is a serious procrastinator."

From the "parts perspective," procrastination is not a character flaw—it is a sign of *internal non-consent*. When parts feel distress, fear, or sadness, it is important to listen to their concerns—not to shame or coerce them into action.* The most effective method of working with your parts (in my opinion) is an evidence-based approach called Internal Family Systems (IFS).† Richard C. Schwartz, founder of IFS, writes: "A part is not just a temporary emotional state or habitual thought pattern . . . it is as if we each contain a society of people, each of whom is at a different age and has different interests, talents, and temperaments."

---

identity disorder. DID is highly stigmatized and misunderstood, but it is a completely reasonable response to severe trauma.

*This perspective doesn't say procrastination is good or that you should avoid challenges. The parts perspective allows you to understand the *function* of procrastination for the purpose of *changing* it.

†There are many therapeutic models besides IFS that use the theory of multiple minds. These include Voice Dialogue, schema therapy, psychosynthesis, hypnotherapy, Gestalt therapy, Structural Dissociation, and ego state therapy.

Think of your parts like a cast of characters. Inside of you are fearful child parts, sullen teenager parts, hungry infant parts, critical parent parts, and more. Often your best attempts at self-care fall flat because you don't know which *part* needs attention. Self-care should really be called *parts* care. A kale smoothie will not comfort an angsty teenager part. A killer Peloton workout will not soothe a lonely child part. When you can identify which character in your "cast" needs your attention, you can more effectively implement solutions. Before choosing a self-care activity, ask yourself:

1. Do I need something that brings my system *up*?
2. Do I need something that brings my system *down*?
3. How old does this part of me feel?
4. What would help this part feel safe, safer, or less threatened?
5. Does this part want alone time or connection with other people?

Behaviors that are self-*care* to one part of you might be self-*harm** to another. Learning to *lead* your internal parts helps you to discern the difference.

Who's in Charge?

Richard Schwartz compares your internal system to an orchestra. An orchestra contains multiple musicians, sections, and instruments. If the musicians decided to sit wherever they wanted and play whatever they wanted, the result would be cacophony. An orchestra conductor is necessary to turn *noise* into *music*. Schwartz writes: "A good conductor has a sense of value of each instrument and the ability of every musician, and is so familiar with music theory that he or she can sense precisely the best point in a symphony to draw out one

---

*Technically, self-harm should be called parts-harm, because self doesn't harm. Parts never have malicious intentions—self-harm is a suboptimal effort to self-protect.

section and mute another . . . this kind of system is (literally) harmonious . . .
Thus, I am suggesting that we all have within us a capable conductor."

The "capable conductor" is known by many different names—the Essential Self, the Higher Self, the Soul, inner wisdom, the Buddha nature, Christ consciousness, Atman, unus mundus, the True Self, the inner teacher, the Holy Spirit, the inner leader . . . and the list goes on. IFS calls the inner leader the Self. Call it whatever you want—the point is that *Self-leadership* is required to manage our shadow impulses and to get unstuck. Self-leadership is the practice of *responding* to stressors rather than *reacting* to triggers.

The goal of therapy (or any inner work) is not to *change* yourself, it's to *know* yourself—and to then conduct your inner orchestra with skill and compassion. We often think of self-compassion as the practice of saying "nice" things about ourselves, but genuine self-compassion is more than that. Genuine self-compassion is a daring quest to know every corner of your inner world. It is a journey to befriend *all* of the parts of yourself. Genuine self-compassion requires you to refuse to abandon even the most shadowy parts of your psyche. Not all *behaviors* are acceptable, but all *parts* are valuable.

As you saw in chapter 3, you aren't lazy and you don't lack motivation—you have *parts* who think the best way to help you is to shut your system down. These parts may act out with destructive behaviors, but the parts themselves aren't bad—their intention is to protect you from your shadows. When your *parts* are in charge, you can feel crazy, out of control, dissociated, indecisive, and overwhelmed. When your inner conductor—your capital *S* Self—is in charge, suddenly you have an all-access pass to what the IFS model calls the 8 C's of Self-Leadership.

THE 8 C'S OF SELF-LEADERSHIP

- ► Confidence
- ► Calmness
- ► Creativity
- ► Clarity
- ► Curiosity

▸ Courage
▸ Compassion
▸ Connectedness

Getting to know your parts can admittedly feel a bit strange in the beginning. My client JD, forty-two, a day trader with a brilliant mind and a proclivity
for self-destruction,* said, "At first doing shadow work was maddening. I felt
like this was going to make me even *more* crazy." During our work together,
he eloquently reflected in his shadow journal (shared with permission):

> Meeting a shadow part was like meeting a child for the first time. I
> wasn't sure how to interact with them and they weren't sure if they
> wanted to interact with me. Once I gained a level of trust with my parts,
> I realized who they were. They are all me, at different moments in my
> life, who have all formed opinions based on how the world and the peo-
> ple in it treated them. Having access to those moments and the person I
> was during those moments allows me to understand myself—I no longer
> sabotage my work, relationships and other areas of my life, because I am
> in touch with the parts of me who only knew how to express themselves
> by breaking stuff—my "little ones" now trust me to take care of things.

The Science of Self-Talk

We talk to ourselves all the time. Often our self-talk is hostile and unhelpful.
Have you ever thought, *OMG, that was so stupid. Why did I say that?* or *I'm so
lazy. How am I supposed to find energy to clean the garage today?* Critical self-talk

---

*Self-destructive should be called parts destructive, since the Self doesn't cause destruction.
And self-sabotage should be called parts protection, since the parts who sabotage are not trying
to harm us—they're trying to *protect* us.

is ineffective and keeps you stuck. If you're thinking, *But I've* tried *self-talk to get myself motivated and it never helps and then I just feel worse*, I hear you. There's a secret to self-talk that makes it work *for* you rather than *against* you. Ready?

The secret to effective self-talk is to turn your inner *monologue* into an inner *dialogue*.

How?

The way to turn your inner monologue into an inner dialogue is to use your name (or your pronouns) when you talk to yourself. Research indicates that changing your self-talk from *first* person (using the word *I*) to *third* person (using your name or pronouns) is a powerful way to shift your system. For example:

First Person: "*I'm* so overwhelmed with everything on my plate."
Third-Person Name: "*Britt* is really overwhelmed with everything on her plate."
Third-Person Pronoun: "*She's* really overwhelmed with everything on her plate."

You can also use second-person language and talk to your parts using the word *you*. When you first start using second- and third-person self-talk, you'll likely feel ridiculous and embarrassed. Why should you even bother with this practice? Viktor E. Frankl wrote: "Between stimulus and response there is a space. In that space is our power to choose our response. In our response lies our growth and our freedom." When you have psychological space between you and your stressors, you are less likely to get stuck. Second- and third-person self-talk helps to create psychological space. There's even a formal term for third-person self-talk: *illeism*. Research lends credibility to this practice.* Per an article in *Scientific Reports*, "[Recent] findings indi-

---

* As with anything, there is a shadow side to illeism. For some people, speaking in the third percate that the language [people] use to refer to the self when they engage in [self-talk] influences self-control. Specifically, using one's own name to refer to the self during introspection, rather than the first-person pronoun 'I,' increases people's ability to control their thoughts, feelings, and behavior under stress."

Why does this practice work? We are generally nicer to other people than we are to ourselves. Talking in third person allows us space to provide the same compassion and kindness to ourselves that we'd extend to others. Disclaimer: It's not enough to simply switch your thoughts from *I* to *he/she/they/you*. Many people continue to beat themselves up using this format. In order to maximize the effectiveness of second- and third-person self-talk, you'll need to apply the principles of Self-parenting to your inner dialogue.

What Is Self-Parenting?

Self-parenting is when you speak to and care for your parts—all of them—with kindness and compassion. John Bradshaw, author of *Homecoming*, wrote: "When you learn how to re-parent yourself, you will stop attempting to complete the past by setting up others to be your parents." When you constantly seek validation from other people or when you push to the point of exhaustion, you're "setting up others to be your parents." When we outsource the job of Self-parenting, we abdicate control of our lives. Without Self-parenting, we stay dependent on *external* sources for *internal* well-being.

The concepts of Self-parenting and inner children can seem saccharine, but as you saw earlier, there's plenty of research to support the validity of compassionate self-talk. (If the idea of inner parents and children doesn't land, you can think of your inner leader as the head coach and replace the

son helps them to distance themselves from personal responsibility. "Shadow illeists" include Gollum, the Hulk, Julius Caesar, and multiple modern-day politicians.

idea of inner children with "inner players" on your "team.") Until we replace the relentless inner *critic* with a compassionate inner *parent*, we tend to spin around in circles. Many people initially resist the idea of Self-parenting. I've heard more than a few clients say, "Self-parenting seems like living in the past and trying to redo childhood. This seems pointless."

Agree.

Self-parenting has nothing to do with your childhood or with blaming your parents. Self-parenting is about *becoming* a parent to your *parts*—even the ones you don't like. This includes what is known as the ego.* You often hear people talk about needing to "kill" the ego. But the ego is a part of your psyche—you don't need to kill it.† Your ego is a necessary and valuable part of your inner society. The ego becomes problematic only in the absence of a skillful inner parent or inner coach. Skillful parents set rules and limits. Skillful parents know how to validate feelings *and* set boundaries.

What does this look like in action?

Imagine you had a horrible week at work, and when you get home Friday evening, you go on a monster food binge. You're lying on the couch feeling miserable and nauseated, but you know that yelling at yourself is pointless—if shame worked, it would have worked by now. You decide to try a compassionate Self-leadership approach:

Instead of thinking: I'm being so bad. God, I suck. I hate that I can't control myself around food. What's *wrong* with me?

Try: Hi, binge part. I know you are hurting right now. I know you were only trying to help me by eating all the food. I didn't take very good care

---

*There are many explanations of the ego. Here's one from the online APA Dictionary of Psychology: "in psychoanalytic theory, ego is the component of the personality that deals with the external world and its practical demands." https://dictionary.apa.org/ego.

†The idea of killing the ego has its place in the esoteric and supra-consciousness realms. Spiritual ego death makes sense. But if we're talking about getting unstuck and integrating parts, trying to kill the ego doesn't work.

of you this week. Next week I will make sure we eat instead of skipping meals and that we take more breaks.

A Self-leadership approach allows you to take psychological space, to form connections with your parts, and to maintain a clear enough head to find solutions. You can remember this method by using the acronym **PART.**

- ► **Pause.** Remember you have multiple parts.
- ► **Acknowledge** your part (or parts) by saying hello.
- ► **Remove** shame from this process—your parts are trying to help you.
- ► **Take** back the "conductor's baton" and make a plan.

If this sounds sentimental and toothless, a more concrete example would be how I (finally) learned to Self-parent my addict parts:

Instead of thinking like this: You are a terrible person.

I learned to think like this: Hi, addict part. I know you were doing the best you could. I appreciate you trying to help me. I'll be honest with you—there are going to be some consequences from these choices, but I'm not going anywhere. You are not bad and I still love you.

Notice how I validated my feelings without excusing or minimizing the behaviors. It is *100 percent* possible to extend kindness to your inner parts while still maintaining boundaries and continuing to take personal responsibility. Many people confuse compassion with permission—but they are not the same. All that said, while Self-parenting is a valuable part of the healing process, it *doesn't* negate the need for other people, professionals,

> Many people confuse compassion with permission—but they are not the same.

or medication. Often we can't access a compassionate inner parent until *after* we've absorbed the benefits from other resources. Self-parenting doesn't replace therapy or medical treatment.

Shadow Snacks

Have you ever tried to ignore a toddler? It doesn't usually fare well. The more you ignore a hungry or overtired child, the louder they scream. As any parent knows, you don't take kids on a trip without bringing snacks. The same is true for your shadow parts. "Shadow snacks" provide a way to manage hungry and overtired inner parts headed for a tantrum.

What are shadow snacks? These are small indulgences you consciously and intentionally permit the destructive parts of yourself to do, think, or have. My play therapy clients are not permitted to throw toys, but I do allow them to say whatever words they want to say—including words typically thought of as bad. When you "feed" small bites to your shadow parts, they feel seen and heard. As soon as shadow parts feel seen and heard, they tend to settle.* The same principle holds for actual children. Many people fear if they even look at their shadow parts—let alone feed them—the shadow will take complete control. The opposite is true. The more we ignore the parts of ourselves we don't like, the harder they fight and the louder they scream. Tending to shadow parts (with boundaries) can soothe their destructive impulses. The character Fear in *Inside Out* was on point when he suggested, "We should lock the door and scream that curse word we know. It's a good one!"

What does feeding your shadow parts snacks look like? Examples of shadow snacks include:†

---

*Feeling seen and heard is not the only reason kids act out. This is one explanation of many.

†Shadow snacking is not the same thing as catharsis. Catharsis is the release of huge amounts of

- ▸ Watching horror or war movies
- ▸ Playing with your food (or better yet, smashing it)
- ▸ Journaling what you'd *really* like to say or do to someone (and then burning the paper)
- ▸ Letting yourself stay in sweats all day
- ▸ Giving yourself permission not to shower
- ▸ Letting yourself doodle or color
- ▸ Playing video games where you can kill things
- ▸ Not answering your phone for a day
- ▸ Allowing yourself to bring the prepackaged veggie tray to the potluck instead of making something yourself
- ▸ Leaving the dishes in the sink

Most of us already do some (or all) of the things on this list. But each of these behaviors is often accompanied by a heavy dose of self-loathing. Shadow snacks are about *conscious*, *intentional*, and even *joyful* indulgences. And just like real snacks, some shadow snacks are nutrient deficient and some are more nutrient dense. A nutrient-deficient shadow snack may "taste" good in the moment—but it comes with negative consequences. Snapping at your spouse instead of screaming at your boss would be a nutrient-*deficient* shadow snack. A nutrient-*dense* shadow snack nurtures your shadow parts while also minimizing consequences.

What's the Healthiest Shadow Snack?

Our *minds* live inside our *brains*, and our *brains* live inside our *bodies*. Because you live in a physical body, the most nutrient-dense shadow snack is *physical*

---

energy, and cathartic practices often backfire. Shadow snacks are small, digestible, and contained actions.

movement. The type of physical movement I'm talking about is not the same as exercise. Using movement as a shadow snack isn't about burning calories or getting six-pack abs, it's about *mindfulness* and *embodiment*.* You don't have to be a professional dancer to access the medicinal benefits of movement. Moving your body shifts breathing and rhythm, which can help send safety signals to your brain.

I remember watching season 6 of *So You Think You Can Dance* either numbed out on Vicodin or spun out on Adderall. One of my favorites was Kathryn McCormick, who currently works as a professional dancer, educator, and Neurosculpting Meditation facilitator. She's also a fellow proponent of Somatic Experiencing. On her website Kathryn writes: "I am learning to nurture all of my parts. I am learning to accept the vast variety of my emotions and the sensations that accompany them . . . I am on a journey of uncovering the wholeness beneath my patterns, habits, and fears."

When I asked her about movement as a way to connect with shadow parts, she told me, "For me, dance is the ultimate check-in. It reveals my subconscious needs and desires. At times what I discover is incredibly uncomfortable. Although I may not enjoy how the sensation feels, I trust that in partnering with movement I have a consistent and natural support system built within me. Movement of any kind, whether it is dance or another art form, creates a safe space that offers inner blockages a pathway to be explored, expressed, and transformed."

When you can "explore, express, and

> Stress is not just in your mind—it is also in your body.

---

*One article defines *embodiment* like this: "We all have bodies and we are always moving, even if it is just breathing. Our movement and body *make visible* all of who we are: our mood, personality, history, family, and culture." Barbara Nordstrom-Loeb, "Embodiment—How to Get It and Why It Is Important." Earl E. Bakken Center for Spirituality and Healing, February 12, 2018. https://www.csh.umn.edu/news-events/blog/thoughts-about-embodiment-how-get-it-and-why -it-important.

transform" shadow content through creative outlets, your inner parts quickly respond. When you feel completely overwhelmed, angry, or anxious, remember that stress is not just in your mind—it is also in your body. Throwing on music and letting your parts move in whatever way they want to is a cost-effective (and time-saving) way to shift out of stuck. Try it for five minutes a day and see what happens after a month of consistent practice.

Conclusion

Poet and philosopher John O'Donohue wrote: "Each inner demon holds a precious blessing that will heal and free you. To receive this gift, you have to lay aside your fear and take the risk of loss and change that every inner encounter offers." Our minds can sometimes go to terrifying and dangerous places, and when this happens, we need other people to help us stay safe. But the thoughts that darken the landscape of your mind are not bad. They are the terrified cries of your internal parts. Refusing to Self-parent our inner children makes it nearly impossible to thrive as adults. Can you achieve success without Self-parenting? Absolutely. Are you free to *enjoy* your success without it? Questionable.

We all have shadowy thoughts that cause us to cringe and think, *Yikes. That wasn't me who just thought that!* But thoughts are not the same as behaviors. You do not have to think positive thoughts all the time. Seeking goodness at the expense of wholeness is costly. The only way to be a good person at all times is to split off from your mind or to lie to yourself or to others. Any healing approaches that value *positivity* over *authenticity* become breeding grounds for *dishonesty*. Wholehearted living requires curiosity and compassion—not denial of our shared humanity. In the children's book *Nothing Sticks Like a Shadow*, the character Rabbit tries desperately to get rid of his shadow—but nothing works. As Rabbit's frustration grows, a wise Raccoon comes along.

"I'm trying to get rid of my shadow," Rabbit said.

"Why?" asked Raccoon. "Shadows are handy things to have. Sometimes they show you where you are going, and sometimes they show you where you've been."

Your shadow is a road map that can lead you home to the one person you need most in the world—yourself.

BOTTOM-LINE TAKEAWAYS

1. *Shadows* refer to any aspects of yourself that you hide or repress.
2. *Shadow work* is the process of being honest *with* yourself *about* yourself.
3. You need your shadow to be whole. Wholeness requires light and darkness.
4. When you hide from your shadow, it gains power and comes out sideways.
5. Your SQ (shadow intelligence) is a measure of your shadow awareness.
6. Every shadow part comes bearing valuable gifts.
7. We all have multiple parts of our personalities.
8. When your inner leader is on board, you can manage even your most destructive and self-defeating behaviors.
9. Talking to yourself in the third person (using your name or pronouns) is more effective than using *I*.
10. Compassion is not the same thing as permission.

DOS AND DON'TS

Do	Don't
Remember that your shadows are neutral until you take action.	Shame yourself for *any* of your thoughts. Thoughts don't become good or bad until they are acted upon.

Do	Don't
Remind yourself (often) that every complex system is made from multiple parts—including your personality.	Call yourself a hypocrite for having opposing thoughts and feelings. Different parts hold different beliefs.
Ask yourself which *part* of your system needs care when you're feeling triggered.	Try to tend to a childlike part with an adultlike intervention.
Talk to yourself using your name or pronouns.	Use *I* statements when talking to yourself.

Five-Minute Challenges

1. Make a list of your inner "cast." Write down as many parts as you can and create a cast list with their ages and descriptions of things they like and dislike.

2. Turn on a three- to five-minute piece of music (close the blinds and turn the lights off if you feel silly) and then let your parts move around in whatever way they want to move.

3. Write a letter *to* a part *from* your inner leader or Self. Then write a letter *from* your part *to* your inner leader. When you write your letter from the part, use your nondominant hand.

4. Make a list of shadow snacks you can have handy when your inner parts feel peckish.

CHAPTER 5

How to Human

Three Crash Courses on Intimacy

"It takes two people to create a pattern, but only one to change it."

—Esther Perel, *Mating in Captivity: Unlocking Erotic Intelligence*

After enduring a long stretch of emotional pyrotechnics in a chaotic and addictive relationship, I finally imploded. What started as a fairy-tale romance devolved into a nightmare of secrets, lies, and intimate partner violence. As a therapist in the addiction rehabilitation world (commonly known as rehab), when I finally broke down/burned out/ spiritually awakened, I was fortunate enough to have access to good help. It didn't matter that I was a therapist and had successfully helped *other* people with their lives. Relationship issues are a great equalizer. We all experience them to a degree. Though you may not experience the levels of depravity to which my own relationships descended, heartbreak is universal. Maya Angelou is quoted as saying, "Love is like a virus. It can happen to anybody at any time." I'll add that when it comes to relational sickness, no one has immunity.

The good news? It doesn't need to take years of therapy (or an advanced degree in traumatology) to shift your relationship out of stuck. Intimacy and trust become possible when you have willing people and accurate information. If you're overwhelmed by the mountain of advice, you're not alone.

Dizzyingly contradictory dos and don'ts fill millions of books, articles, pod-casts, blogs, and magazines:

> *8 Tricks to Drive Him Wild with Desire!*
> *It's Not YOUR Job to Satisfy HIM. Do These 5 Things Instead.*
> *Why Space Is Healthy for Your Relationship!*
> *Why Too Much Space Is Toxic for Your Relationship.*
> *Scheduling Sex Can Put the Spice Back in Your Marriage—Do It!*
> *Scheduling Sex Takes All the Spontaneity Out of Your Marriage—Don't Do It!*

Facepalm. Any wonder that so many relationships are either stuck or pronounced dead on arrival? Though there are countless resources that focus on intimacy issues, you need only a few basic pieces of information to get unstuck. This chapter divides and organizes the basics into three crash courses. Each one is a synthesis of academic journals, scientific research, noted authors, my own clinical experiences, and evidence-based best practices in psychotherapy. If you're seriously strapped for time, skip to the section on Apologies vs. Amends.

How to Human—Three Crash Courses on Intimacy

In Crash Course 1 (Conflict Languages), you'll learn why your conversations derail, and discover a simple work-around. In Crash Course 2 (Boundaries), you'll find out the difference between boundaries and requests. Why does that matter? The difference between setting a boundary and making a request is the difference between a simple two-minute conversation and a marathon knock-down, drag-out fight. Finally, Crash Course 3 (Apologies vs. Amends) provides a detailed script for how to repair a relationship misstep. Spoiler alert: Relational repair does *not* include the words "I'm sorry."

Sound like a lot of work? It is—initially. If you're a skeptic (or just exhausted), you may sigh and ask, "Well, why bother?" The answer—it takes *way* more work to *avoid* the work than to *do* the work. As Harville Hendrix, a world-renowned couple therapist and author of *Getting the Love You Want*, puts it: "We are prisoners of the fear of change. Couples . . . would rather divorce, break up the family, and divide up all their possessions than acquire a new style of relating."

But What If My Partner Won't Do the Work with Me?

It is next to impossible to conjure willingness in an unwilling partner. Begging, pleading, ignoring, screaming, avoiding, bargaining, threatening—the list of what we've *all* tried goes on and on. And yet never in the history of ever has yelling at someone *louder* caused them to listen to and understand us *better*. You might ask, "But what if my partner won't read the books/do the exercises/go to therapy/[fill in the blank]?"

I hear you.

Rather than attempting to change what your *partner* is doing, your power lies in the decision to change how you *respond* to what they are doing. If your partner is not willing to approach things with a different mindset, the only pattern you can change is the status of the relationship, *not* the way in which you two relate. But that's another topic altogether. If your partner is also sick and tired of feeling stuck and is willing to at least *try* something new, invite them to join us for Crash Course 1.

Crash Course 1: Conflict Languages

There's a famous Buddhist saying that you can apply to intimacy: "Pain is inevitable, suffering is optional." Said another way, conflict is inevitable, but *fighting* is optional. A *conflict language* is a system of communication that creates safety during difficult conversations. As we learned in chapter 3, a brain stuck in survival mode does not think clearly and logically. Once your brain perceives danger, the gloves come off and punches fly. In order to stay in "thinking brain," we need safety hacks to prevent amygdala hijack* (overwhelm). In *Wired for Love,* Dr. Stan Tatkin writes: "Devote yourself to your partner's sense of safety and security and not simply to your idea of what that should be. What may make you feel safe and secure may not be what your partner requires from you. Your job is to know what matters to your partner and how to make him or her feel safe and secure."

What are some examples of a conflict language? Some people prefer to talk at night and others first thing in the morning. Some people prefer to sit next to each other during conflict and others want more physical space. Big companies use these strategies religiously. A human resources director would *never* randomly storm up to an employee waiting in line at Starbucks and angrily spit, "You're always the first one to leave for coffee. You never think about anyone else. And why are you always late to senior staff meetings? I hate you. I'm going to fire you. But don't leave the company. We really do love you. But I don't see how this can work. Forget this. Just forget it."

Doesn't that sound strange? (Not to mention a lawsuit waiting to happen.) And yet how often do we pounce on our partners the second they walk through the door? How often do we raise our voices and say things we wish we could take back? How quickly do *your* fights escalate from talking about one thing to talking about *all* the things?

In *The Five Love Languages*, Dr. Gary Chapman writes: "Recent research has indicated that the average individual listens for only seventeen seconds before interrupting and interjecting his own ideas." This means if you

---

* "We have two amygdala, one on each side of the brain, behind the eyes and the optical nerves. Dr. Bessel van der Kolk, in his book *The Body Keeps the Score,* calls this the brain's 'smoke detector.' It's responsible for detecting fear and preparing our body for an emergency response." Diane Musho Hamilton, "Calming Your Brain During Conflict," December 22, 2015. https://hbr .org/2015/12/calming-your-brain-during-conflict.

haven't made your point in seventeen seconds, then it's game, set, match. Checkmate. Case closed.

Dr. Chapman's work on love languages teaches people to learn their partners' preferences for receiving affection. He identifies five distinct types: words of affirmation, acts of service, quality time, physical touch, and gifts. Knowing your partner's love language can make it easier to show and receive affection.

If you're like most people, you cannot even *imagine* using love languages when your anger meter shoots into the red. In *Things I Wish I'd Known Before We Got Married*, Dr. Chapman writes: "People do not get married planning to divorce. Divorce is the result of lack of preparation for marriage and the failure to learn the skills of working together as teammates in an intimate relationship." While tender expressions of love are a beautiful ideal, it seems that languages of *conflict* are needed first. I've identified six.

THE SIX CONFLICT LANGUAGES

1. Social Distancing	The 2020 quarantine might be over, but less than six feet of distance can still feel dangerous, at least emotionally. Leave lots of room to wander during conflict and easy access to the door. This helps prevent the brain from feeling threatened.
2. Time Limits	In chess this would be called an adjournment. Take frequent breaks. Set a timer. When the time is up, do not return to the conversation for at least a few hours (or until the next day). This allows lengthy conversations to proceed at a sustainable pace.
3. Virtual vs. In-Person	Some people (especially abuse survivors) get triggered if they are in the same room during a conflict. While fighting over text is not recommended, Zoom, FaceTime, or phone calls are totally acceptable methods of communication.
4. Emergency Exit	In the BDSM world, "safe words" are used to immediately stop the action if someone feels threatened or changes their mind. The same technique can be applied to difficult conversations to ensure consent.

5. Food Fights	It is almost impossible to eat and scream at the same time. This is because when our fight-or-flight-or-freeze alarm is triggered, digestion goes off-line. Agreeing to have difficult conversations while eating a meal uses the science of the survival brain to prevent escalation.
6. Geographic Location	Making geographic decisions on the front end can increase safety and decrease intensity. Fighting in a car can quickly turn dangerous, since there is no way to escape. Facing each other, sitting side by side, consciously choosing what room in which to hold the conversation, what furniture to sit on . . . These decisions can improve safety dramatically.

What if your conflict language is different from your partner's conflict language? In this next section, you'll take these six conflict languages and customize them for your own relationship using a conflict contract.

Conflict Contracts

You don't buy a house without a contract. You don't hire a lawyer without a contract. You don't sign up for a gym membership without a contract. And yet after a marriage is finalized, the idea of a relationship contract is never brought up again—unless you land in divorce court. Movies, television, and pop culture normalize and even glamorize fighting. We mistakenly believe that fights don't require a playbook, sportsmanship, or guidelines.

They do.

A *conflict contract* is a document that clearly specifies the rules for fair fighting. You wouldn't expect Tom Brady to march off the field mid-game, cross his arms, and mumble, "I'm too mad to play." The difference between a football game and a bar brawl is the presence of an arena, a rule book, and time limits. Even the fiercest opponents in a boxing match do not enter the ring unless they first agree to a code of conduct. The athletic world is relentless in its efforts to maintain safety during high-octane intensity. Yet we enter into arguments with our loved ones without even the degree of consideration seen during sportsball games. Denise and Bryan, a successful professional couple, are a great example of how the absence of a strategy quickly turns into the presence of fireworks:

Denise, an energetic and cheerful forty-seven-year-old, and Bryan, a fifty-one-year-old who runs six miles a day and dreams of owning multiple businesses, are co-owners of a popular doggie day spa. Denise and Bryan are the definition of a powerhouse couple. Their strategic Facebook posts show countless pictures of happy teenagers, Pinterest-perfect home decor, and extravagant family vacations. It didn't take long to see the chaos behind the curtain. They stormed into my office and it was game on. She accused him. He raised his voice at her. She hurled a series of expletives at him. He turned purple and gripped my couch so hard the leather nearly ripped. I rose from my chair and regretfully told them we needed to end the session immediately because this was a waste of both *their* money and *my* time. Startled into silence, these intelligent and capable adults suddenly looked like sheepish little kids. As their trauma responses (internal alarms) turned off, their capacity for thoughtful discussion returned. Before they could even land *near* a solution, Bryan and Denise needed to first construct a conflict contract.

What is a conflict contract?

A conflict contract is a written document that you and your partner(s) create and sign *before* the waves crash down on the relationship. As is true in any athletic rivalry, the way to work through intense conflict without below-the-belt sucker punches is to first create a rule book for *how* to talk. Once you nail down the how, then you can safely move on to who did what to whom. In the book *Nonviolent Communication*, author Marshall Rosenberg says, "We are dangerous when we are not conscious of our responsibility for how we behave, think and feel." Creating a conflict contract helps you to stay conscious so you don't end up speaking words you later regret.

When enough emotional space is present for you to breathe, think, and make choices, you can quickly get past long-standing patterns of stuck. At the first sign of conflict, retrieve the contract and review the terms of the talk. If you cannot or will not abide by the terms, disengage. You'd be amazed how effectively this technique prevents major blowouts.

There is some debate in the academic field about the effectiveness of relationship contracts. Some experts recommend contracts and others caution against their use. However, these disagreements refer to contracts that focus on conversation topics such as the frequency of sex, chore allocation, in-law visits, the scheduling of date nights, and gift-giving standards. In contrast, this crash course encourages you to focus your contract solely on conflict negotiation.

Research confirms that when we get angry, our brains shift from logical to irrational. Loving partners morph into hostile adversaries when our brains shift into irrational mode. When your rational brain turns off, it is pointless to attempt rational discussion. Without a predetermined agreement, the likelihood that we will stay cemented to our old patterns is high. Denise and Bryan's conflict contract looked like this:

THIS CONTRACT IS ENTERED INTO BY DENISE AND BRYAN, NOW KNOWN AS THE COUPLE, ON THIS 4TH DAY OF APRIL. THE COUPLE AGREES TO THE FOLLOWING TERMS AND CONDITIONS OF CONFLICT:

- THE COUPLE agrees that any disagreements will be scheduled via Outlook meeting invites.
- THE COUPLE agrees that disagreement conversations will not take place within 24 hours of a holiday/birthday/major event.
- THE COUPLE agrees that conversations will alternate between in person and Zoom.
- THE COUPLE agrees that disputes be held in the family room, with Denise occupying the gray armchair and Bryan occupying the ottoman. Both parties agree to maintain at least 10 feet of space between them at all times.

- THE COUPLE agrees that any disputes can take place only if ALL of the children are out of the house.
- THE COUPLE agrees that any argument that exceeds 30 minutes will immediately be paused for a one-hour break. If the argument is not resolved within 60 minutes, then both parties agree to resume after a 24-hour break.
- THE COUPLE agrees that if one or both parties is unwilling to adhere to the terms of the contract, he/she will immediately agree to terminate the conversation and try again in 24 hours.

Does this sound ridiculous? Using a conflict contract can definitely feel clumsy and awkward. The creation of such a contract requires time and effort on the front end, but the return on investment is high. In *The 7 Habits of Highly Effective People*, author Stephen Covey coaches us to consider what is *important* rather than what is *urgent*. In this case, what is most important is crafting the *structure* for disagreement before diving into the *content* of the disagreement, no matter how urgent.

Knowing how to *navigate* conflict is good. Knowing how to *minimize* conflict is better. Knowing how to *prevent* conflict is best. Robert Frost said, "Good fences make good neighbors." This idea can also be applied to intimacy. Good plans make good partners. In a healthy relationship, you know your own limits and respect the limits of your partner. This requires a working understanding of boundaries, which we'll discuss next, in Crash Course 2.

Crash Course 2: Boundaries

What is a boundary? A boundary is a physical or metaphorical border that separates two or more things. The ocean's edge is a boundary between land and sea. Your skin is a boundary between the external world and your internal organs, cells, and tissues. A wall is a boundary that separates rooms. In relationships, boundaries are your *limits*. Your boundaries mark the edges of your tolerance and willingness. Frustration, resentment, and feeling taken for granted are all telltale signs of boundary trouble.

Authors across a wide range of disciplines and spiritual orientations agree about boundaries:

- "Those people in our lives who can respect our boundaries will love our wills, our opinions, our separateness. Those who can't respect our boundaries are telling us that they don't love our nos. They only love our yesses, our compliance." Dr. Henry Cloud and Dr. John Townsend, *Boundaries: When to Say Yes, How to Say No to Take Control of Your Life* (biblically based Christian self-help)

- "Before you enter a room with people, set your intention to protect your energy and create healthy boundaries." Gabrielle Bernstein, spiritual self-help author of *The Universe Has Your Back: Transform Fear to Faith*

- "To set good boundaries takes a lot of courage . . . but the intention is to make communication clearer." Pema Chödrön, author and Buddhist nun

- "When we fail to set boundaries and hold people accountable, we feel used and mistreated." Dr. Brené Brown, research professor and author of five number-one *New York Times* bestsellers

- "A healthy boundary creates controlled vulnerability." Pia Mellody, clinical fellow at the Meadows of Wickenburg, Arizona, and recovery expert

- "'No' is a complete sentence." Anne Lamott, essayist and author

Boundaries allow partners to manage expectations. Why is this important? The space between expectations and reality is the birthplace of resentment. There are many types of boundaries (sexual, financial, physical, emotional, conversational, etc.), but for this crash course we'll focus on the very first thing you need to get a relationship out of stuck—behavioral boundaries.

Behavioral Boundaries

The biggest misconception about boundaries is that they require someone *else* to agree with you. This is false. Boundaries are not about making others do things. People often think they're setting a boundary, but what they're really doing is making a request. When you say, "They keep crossing my boundaries!" what you likely mean is "They didn't do what I wanted them to do!" The difference between a boundary and a request, as you might recall from earlier in the chapter, is the difference between a short conversation and a marathon argument. A *request* is when you ask someone to do something. The power to say yes or no lies with the person to whom you make the request. The floor is wide open for debate and argument. A *boundary* is a choice *you* make in response to *their* behavior. No discussion needed. Boundaries *never* require input or compliance from another person.

For example, you might try to set a boundary with your wife that you want to get to the airport two hours ahead of departure. She likes to leave for the airport at the last second, but you hate feeling rushed. Asking her to leave early is a request. A boundary would be to tell her, "If you choose not to leave for the airport on time, I will choose to take an Uber early and meet you there." Boundaries are all about *you* and *your* choices; they never depend on another person doing what you want them to do. Letting a person know that if they choose X, you will choose Y—that is a boundary.

Requests	Behavioral Boundaries
"I'd really prefer if you call to let me know you are running late."	"If you choose to not let me know your expected time home, I will choose to not prepare extra food."
"I really don't like it when you drink three bottles of wine at night. Please stop doing that."	"If you choose to drink more than one bottle of wine at night, I will choose to sleep in another bedroom."
"It's frustrating to me when you make plans at the last second. I really want you to give me more notice."	"I need to have at least three days' notice for plans. If you choose not to give me time to plan, then I will choose to say no."
"Your friend Kevin is a jerk. I don't want to be in the same room with him."	"I respect that Kevin is your friend. If you choose to invite him to the party, I will choose not to go to the party."

"Hold on a second," you might protest. "These sound an awful lot like ultimatums!"

No one likes ultimatums. The biggest difference between a boundary and an ultimatum is *intent*.

> Boundaries are all about you and your choices.

Ultimatums are about power and control and relationship *domination*. Boundaries are about safety and space and relationship *preservation*. Ultimatums sound like this: "If you don't have sex with me five times a week, I am going to cheat on you." A good way to tell the difference is to simply ask yourself if your intention is to stay present and grounded in your *mind* or to force behavioral changes on your *partner*.

If someone threatens, screams, blocks your path, or in any way prohibits you from setting and enforcing your boundaries, that is not crossing boundaries—that is abuse. Abuse is not the focus of this chapter, but I'll say quickly that it is not a relationship problem. Or a communication problem. The only person responsible for abuse is the abuser, period. Most relationship advice does *not* apply to abusive situations, and couples therapy is almost *never* recommended if one of the partners is abusive.

Before you start worrying that your relationship might be abusive, remind yourself that even the healthiest relationships have the occasional suboptimal moments. A bad blowup now and then does not necessarily mean the relationship is toxic. If you and your partner(s) are willing to own your mistakes and try again (see Crash Course 3), then no need to panic. The more you practice boundaries *before* the pot boils over, the faster you'll get out of relationship hot water. In *The Relationship Cure,* relationship expert John Gottman writes: "Connecting is not magic. Like any other skill, it can be learned, practiced, and mastered."

A word of caution: You know that sore feeling when you first start a workout program? Everything aches, nothing feels natural, and you need to remind yourself that making a good decision doesn't always immediately produce a good result? Yes, *that* feeling. Boundaries are the same. Setting boundaries can feel awful when you first try to do so, but do it anyway. Learning to set boundaries is like building muscle strength. You wouldn't expect to do twenty pull-ups without training and practice. Do not shame yourself. If you're not used to thinking about boundaries as a self-care strategy, your brain will likely confuse self-*care* behavior with self*ish* behavior.

Every boundary-setting beginner feels mean and selfish for a short time. *Feeling* mean and selfish is not the same thing as *acting* mean and selfish. *Selfish* people withhold affection and care. The fact that you're worried about being selfish means it is highly unlikely that you *are* selfish. Boundaries are about creating temporary space. The intention with boundaries is to maintain a sense of safety and calm so you can return to the conversation fully prepared to give your best. And when things go off the rails (which they will) and you screw it up (as we all do from time to time), the repair process is *way* more effective when you use *amends* rather than *apologies*. Crash Course 3 explains the difference—and why it matters.

Crash Course 3: Apologies vs. Amends

The point of an apology is to recognize hurt feelings, express regret about the mistake or misunderstanding, and provide a plan for avoiding a repeat. Yet the phrase "I'm sorry" conveys *none* of that. Merriam-Webster defines the word *sorry* as "feeling sorrow." Umm . . . sorrow about what? Sorrow about getting caught? Sorrow that a long-winded emotional conversation is suddenly necessary? "I'm sorry" is an empty phrase at best and rapidly turns toxic when the word *if* is thrown into the mix. Putting these words together is the ultimate exercise in how *not* to human.

- ► I'm sorry *IF* you were hurt.
- ► I'm sorry *IF* you took things the wrong way.
- ► I'm sorry *IF* you don't like what I did.
- ► I'm sorry *IF* you feel angry.
- ► I'm sorry *IF* . . .

Have any of these phrases ever made *you* feel understood, seen, validated, and secure in your relationship?

Me neither.

Rather than offering apologies, making *amends* is the fastest path out of stuck in a relationship. Making amends is a concept from the Twelve-Step addiction recovery model. While I have issues with some of the practices of the Twelve-Step program, the concept of amends as opposed to apologies is one to which I fully subscribe. Making amends is appropriate whether you identify as an addict or not. The Hazelden Betty Ford Foundation, one of the original addiction recovery organizations, says, "Think of amends as actions taken that demonstrate your new way of life . . . whereas apologies are basically words. When you make amends, you acknowledge and align your values to your actions by admitting wrongdoing and then living by your principles." Apologies don't accomplish the goals of acknowledgment or alignment. The phrase "I'm sorry" is often hollow and devoid of meaning.

Yet we're all taught from early childhood that when we hurt someone we're supposed to say "I'm sorry."

Saying "I'm sorry" does the trick when you step on someone's foot or forget to refill the water in the Keurig. Apologies are great for simple mistakes and as common courtesy. Deeper relational cuts require something stronger than an apology, which brings us to the topic of *amends*. Amends-making is a potent way to cauterize wounds. I use a method I call the Four O's. You'll notice that the words *I'm sorry* are conspicuously absent. Implementing this tool can save you hours of therapy and thousands of dollars. Following this script *dramatically* decreases the need for lengthy and circular conversations.

HOW TO MAKE AMENDS: THE FOUR O'S

1	OWN your behavior. *("I admit I did/didn't . . .")*
2	OBSERVE how your behavior impacted your partner. *("I imagine you must have felt . . .")*
3	OUTLINE your plan not to do the behavior again. *("In the future I will prevent this by . . .")*
4	OFFER to listen if they need to share anything else about your behavior. *("Is there anything else you need me to know about how this impacted you? I'm willing to listen.")*

What does this look like in action? Let's say Esa is an accountant with a major filing deadline. Earlier in the week, her wife, Davey, promised to watch the kids Saturday morning so that Esa could work. Saturday morning arrives. Davey runs out to Costco and loses track of time, and Esa's day is quickly swallowed by the feeding, cleaning, and entertaining required by their two young children and rambunctious chocolate Lab. A baseline apology would be for Davey to simply say, "I'm sorry I was late." A toxic apology would be if she said, "Well, I had things to do too. I'm sorry if you missed your deadlines, but that's just the way it goes."

Neither baseline nor toxic apologies convey empathy. Stay in a relationship long enough and you'll likely end up on the giving and receiving side of both. Before I learned this information, my apologies were more of a knee-jerk effort to avoid feeling guilty rather than an attempt at genuine relationship repair. Can you relate?

Instead of apologizing, if Davey offered Esa an *amends*, it would sound like this:

1. I totally lost track of time and did not keep my promise to watch the kids. (***OWN***)
2. I imagine you must have felt angry, confused, betrayed, and scared about missing your deadline. (***OBSERVE***)
3. In the future, I will not try to squeeze in my own to-do list when I commit to doing something for you. (***OUTLINE***)
4. Is there anything you need me to know about how this impacted you? I'm willing to listen. (***OFFER***)

Using this technique accomplishes several tasks:

▸ You validate to your partner that they are not crazy—the thing they are upset about *did* happen because of *your* action.
▸ Using an empathy statement allows your partner to feel seen and heard. This creates a bridge for deep healing and repair. It also decreases limbic (emotional) brain activity and allows for reasonable and logical communication.
▸ You are accountable for creating a plan so you don't repeat the problem.
▸ Your partner can feel secure because now they know you have a plan to prevent the problem.
▸ Offering to actively listen prevents the buildup of resentment and creates space for intimacy and repair.

What about situations where the conflict is caused by a misunderstanding? The Four O's work beautifully for misunderstandings because they don't require self-flagellation or admission of wrongdoing. Let's return to Davey and Esa. This time, imagine that Davey *hadn't* agreed to cover childcare and did *not* know about Esa's deadline. On Saturday morning, Davey runs out to Costco and returns in the afternoon, and Esa misses her deadline. Technically Davey hasn't done anything "wrong," but as a loving partner she still wants to support Esa's feelings. In that case, Davey could use the Four O's this way:

1. My decision to stay out running errands resulted in your missing your deadline. (***OWN:** Notice that Davey is providing objective data. She is naming the impact her behavior had on Esa. She is not apologizing or taking on the burden of guilt.*)

2. I imagine you must have felt frustrated and scared about missing your deadline. (***OBSERVE:** Regardless of our intentions, this step allows us to see how our actions impact others. With empathy statements, we do not need to defend or justify our behavior.*)

3. In the future, I'll check in with you before leaving on Saturday mornings. (***OUTLINE:** This step acknowledges that better communication can prevent this from recurring.*)

4. Is there anything you need me to know about how this impacted you? I'm willing to listen. (***OFFER:** Most people appreciate the opportunity to be better understood.*)

Davey isn't apologizing for wrongdoing. She's not taking ownership of an error because none exists. What Davey *is* doing, however, is providing reassurance to Esa by owning, observing, outlining, and offering.

Making amends initially feels awkward. I've had more than a few clients complain, "This is weird. No one talks like this." It's true—no one is *taught* to talk like this. It is not a normal way to converse. But how effective is what

> We need a new normal to get out of stuck.

we call the normal way? Judging by the rapidly increasing need for mental health professionals, it seems that we need a new normal to get out of stuck. When I worked at an inpatient drug rehab in Arizona, clients spent hours role-playing boundaries and amends. One of my favorite clients was Alex, a recovering addict in his early twenties. Alex had zero patience and a hot temper. During his first few weeks in the program, he'd growl during group therapy and snap, "Britt, this is the *dumbest* way of talking that I've ever heard." By the time he completed treatment he was nine months sober, back in school, and working part-time at a construction job he really enjoyed. A few months after he left Arizona, he sent me a text that still makes me smile:

> *Hey it's Alex. I'm sober and doing really good. You know that stupid exercise we all had to do where we did that amends thing? Yeah, it works. It totally works. I still hate it though.*

Bottom-Line Takeaways

1. You can't change your partner, but you *can* change how you respond to them.
2. When you know your conflict language, you're more likely to stay in control during arguments.
3. Conflict is inevitable; *fighting* is optional.
4. Creating a conflict contract can help build a safe container for arguments.
5. If you and your partner(s) are not willing to follow the conflict contract, disengage.
6. A request is when you ask someone *else* to do something. The power to do it or not do it lies with *them*.
7. A boundary is what *you* choose to do in response to someone else. The power to do it or not do it lies with *you*.

8. Boundaries *never* depend on another person doing what you want them to do.
9. Making amends is more effective than saying "I'm sorry."
10. There are four parts to making amends: *Own* the thing you did; *Observe* how it impacted your partner; *Outline* your plan not to do it again; *Offer* to listen.

DOS AND DON'TS

Do	Don't
Make sure you are well rested, fed, and hydrated before trying to engage in conflict.	Have an argument when you are sleep-deprived, hungry, or thirsty.
Think of the ways you feel safest when arguing. In person? Over a meal? Via Zoom?	Try to engage in conflict until you both come to an agreement about the rules first.
Say "I'm sorry" for minor things.	Say "I'm sorry" for major things. Use the Four O's of amends-making instead.
Ask your partner if they are willing to participate with conflict contracts, amends, and boundaries.	Be passive-aggressive by leaving this chapter bookmarked on your partner's nightstand in hopes they will get the hint.

FIVE-MINUTE CHALLENGE

1. Copy the Four O's chart into a notebook. Then practice it on
   your partner(s) with something minor. For example:

1	OWN the thing you did. *("I admit I did/didn't . . .")*
I admit that I left the dishes in the sink.	

2	OBSERVE how your behavior impacted your partner. *("I imagine you must have felt . . .")*
I imagine you must have felt frustrated.	

3	OUTLINE your plan not to do the thing again. *("In the future I will prevent this by . . .")*
In the future I will set my alarm fifteen minutes earlier so I have time to clean the kitchen.	

4	OFFER to listen if they need to share anything you missed. *("Is there anything else you need me to know about how this impacted you? I'm willing to listen.")*
Is there anything else about this situation you want me to know?	

CHAPTER 6

The Sticky World of Friendships and Dating

On Wednesdays we wear pink.

—Karen Smith, *Mean Girls*

ell hath no fury like a clique of fifth graders. Especially if the clique is a stereotypical group of Long Island girls. Brutal.

The Tackan Elementary School bus stop was the site of daily humiliation. Each morning I'd pray that the bus would arrive quickly. For years I'd stand there clutching my books while the mean-girl clique huddled together gossiping. Occasionally one of them would look over at me and shoot me an icy glare or an evil cackle. Rainy days were the worst. Alicia, the ringleader (and my nemesis all the way through high school), would invite the girls into her house so they could stay dry and warm until the bus arrived. I'd stand under the corner stop sign and they'd watch from the house as I got soaked. Then there was that fateful day they stole my sticker book. If you were born after 1990, you may be unfamiliar with these prized childhood relics. Before Minecraft, Roblox, and Disney Plus, we had sticker books—empty photo albums in which to house sticker collections. Mine was my pride and joy, full of colorful unicorns from Lisa Frank (no relation), fuzzies, oilies, and scratch 'n' sniffs. Every now and then I'd get to go to the sticker store and choose a few that I'd carefully add to my book. Care Bears, Rainbow Brite, Strawberry Shortcake . . . I absolutely adored my sticker collection. Then one blustery and snowy day at the bus stop, Alicia grabbed it out of my hands, threw it into a giant slush puddle, and then laughed as it sank.

Why am I sharing this story?

Friendships are tricky at every stage. Women are taught to hate, fear, loathe, envy, compare, and destroy other women from early childhood—and the dynamics don't really change as we get older. The cafeteria battle zone evolves into carpool mama drama. Prom queen pressure evolves into a game of "Who will win PTA president?" Adult friendships can feel elusive and ephemeral. Believe me, I get it. It wasn't until I hit my midthirties that I understood the medicinal magic of relationships.

Friendships are not a luxury; they are as important to your health as fresh water and clean air. The 2020 pandemic shone a piercing spotlight on the consequences of loneliness and isolation. As venerable author C. S. Lewis poetically but erroneously stated in *The Four Loves*, "Friendship is unnecessary, like philosophy, like art . . . it has no survival value; rather it is one of those things which give value to survival." Science shows that friendship actually *does* have survival value. Dr. Brené Brown writes in *The Gifts of Imperfection*, "We are biologically, cognitively, physically, and spiritually wired to love, be loved, and to belong. When those needs are not met, we don't function as we were meant to be . . . the absence of love and belonging will always lead to suffering." Even though science repeatedly validates friendships as essential for healthy living, the idea that friends are anything more than a fluffy frivolity can be a hard sell. Suggesting that friendship is a biological imperative is an *especially* hard sell to a room of exclusively female C-level executives—the most formidable group to whom I ever presented a keynote.

The penthouse of the shiny high-rise hummed with powerful networking energy as brilliant and beautiful women began to gather. As for me? I was huddled in a bathroom trying not to throw up, frantically texting my therapist, and wiping sweat off my shaking palms. Decades of "women are mean" messages raced through my head. It took every brain hack in my arsenal (see chapter 3) to remind myself that this was *not* the corner bus stop and I was no longer the small child waiting in exile for my ride to school. Note: If you can relate to the experience of suddenly feeling small, overwhelmed, and younger than your chronological age, we'll cover emotional regression in chapter 9.

The title of my talk? "The Science of Social Engagement: Why Friendship Is Not Optional." With fifty steely eyes trained on me skeptically, I stood up straight, faked a smile, and began the presentation. I saw a few eyebrows raise in curiosity at some shocking statistics from a *Harvard Women's Health Watch* article: "One study, which examined data from more than 309,000 people, found that lack of strong relationships increased the risk of premature death from all causes by 50%—an effect on mortality risk roughly comparable to smoking up to 15 cigarettes a day, and greater than obesity and physical inactivity."* The energy of the room began to shift. Murmurs of surprise amplified when they heard about Susan Pinker, TED speaker and award-winning author, psychologist, and social science columnist for *The Wall Street Journal*. Pinker writes in *The Village Effect* that "neglecting to keep in close contact with people who are important to you is at least as dangerous to your health as a pack-a-day cigarette habit, hypertension, or obesity."

Finally the room cracked open. As arms uncrossed and stoic faces relaxed into smiles, a deep and intimate conversation ensued. Heads nodded vigorously and a few of the women even laughed as we commiserated about the relentless inner critic, impostor syndrome, and nagging feelings of loneliness common to *everyone*. One of the attendees, Dr. Michelle Robin, a highly esteemed author/speaker/wellness warrior, eventually became a good friend. On one of our walk-and-talks the following spring, she said, "Everyone talks about exercise as a factor of health, but we need reminders about the other things that are also important."

Friendship is a health necessity, not something to toss to the bottom of the priority pile. If you struggle to find friends, this chapter will spotlight three crucial pieces of information you'll need to get unstuck. If you have a friend group with whom you constantly feel frustration, this chapter will help

---

*Harvard Health Publishing, "The Health Benefits of Strong Relationships." Staying Healthy, December 1, 2010.

you understand why and give you a new way to think about your social connections. Since the dynamics of friendship are similar to the dynamics of dating, you can also apply the principles of friend-finding to the dating world.

There are plenty of books and resources on *why* it is important to have friends. There are plenty of blog posts and podcasts that suggest *how* to find friends. And yet often our friendship goals remain confined to the realm of wishful thinking. This is because the literature on friendships focuses mostly on why and how and largely ignores *what*. What constitutes an adult friendship? What roles do you want friends to play? What toxic friendship myths have crept into your belief systems? The answers to these questions are key to unlocking a satisfying social life and make up what I call the Three D's of Friend-Finding:

1. *Differences* between childhood and adulthood friendships
2. *Defining* the roles we want our friends to play
3. *Deconstructing* the six myths of friendship

Differences Between Childhood and Adulthood Friendships

During a play therapy session, one of my seven-year-old clients was hard at work in the dollhouse. She paused, took a pensive look at the little plastic girls on the miniature couch, and then pointedly told me, "Amy is my best friend. But Braelyn is my *best* best friend. I tell her *everything*. And we're gonna be friends until we're old like you!"

A cognitive (thought) distortion that keeps many of us stuck is the idea that childhood friendships and adult friendships operate by the same rules. They don't. Friendships in childhood are easier because—excluding oppressive factors such as poverty—the adulting is done by adults. Children don't have to worry about mortgage payments, meal prep, and rush-hour traffic. Children also have the benefit of the *proximity principle*, a term coined by social scientists. This principle states that attraction is largely predicted by frequency and proximity. Children, adolescents, and even college kids see one another daily in class and around the neighborhood or on campus. These encounters greatly mitigate barriers to friendships. The following chart illustrates important distinctions between childhood and adulthood friendships.

CHILDHOOD VS. ADULTHOOD FRIENDSHIPS

Childhood Friendships	Adulthood Friendships
No worries about adulting.	*All* the worries about adulting.
We see each other EVERY DAY!	Get-togethers are infrequent and often difficult to schedule.
We fight like siblings but always make up in the end!	Healthy adult friendships may experience *conflict* but do not need to include *fights*. If you're fighting often with a friend, it might be time to reevaluate the friendship.
We will be friends FOREVER!	Adult friendships organically fade in and out over time.
My best friend and I tell each other EVERYTHING!	Boundaries about what to share, when, and with whom are crucial to maintain emotional safety.

Most of us aren't taught how to navigate friendship dynamics as adults, so it makes sense that we'd stay stuck. When you give yourself permission to redefine friendship, you broaden your target and increase your likelihood of hitting the mark. Here's what permission looks like for me. Feel free to take what's useful and add your own:

- ▸ I give myself permission to see my friends infrequently.
- ▸ I give myself permission to accept the reality that friendships fade in and out over time.
- ▸ I give myself permission to enjoy different levels of friendships, not just "besties."

▸ I give myself permission to disengage from any friendships that continue to be high conflict.

▸ I give myself permission to leave early from gatherings.

▸ I give myself permission to not participate in friendships that drain my energy.

▸ I give myself permission to say no to baby showers, weddings, and engagement parties.

Imagine the possibilities. With permission to approach your friendships from a place of *authenticity* rather than how you think or wish things should look, you free yourself from the pit of resentment. What might open up if you allowed yourself to authentically and bravely define friendship for *yourself*? It may look totally different from what appears normal. Some of my favorite people in the world are those whom I see only once a year. But even when our contact is this infrequent, the time we spend together fills my tank. I call these my "scorpion friends." Scorpions eat one-third of their body weight in just one meal and can easily go a year without food. Scorpion friends work for me because I'm a hard-core introvert and require an inordinate amount of alone time. You might crave daily contact with friends, so scorpion friendships would *not* work. (Hummingbirds need to eat daily. So you may find hummingbird friends a suitable alternative.)

Once you grant yourself permission to custom-tailor friendship *rules*, it is time to consider *roles*. All the research on how to find friends and why we need them is useful to a point. But if you don't know what *specific* roles your friends are available to play, then you'll likely end up frustrated. Think of a Hollywood casting director. They need to *first* consider the role and *then* ensure the actor is an appropriate fit. In his memoir *Love Life*, actor Rob Lowe* writes, "I think it was Alfred Hitchcock who said that 90% of successful movie making is in the casting. The same is true in life."

---

*Rob Lowe is forever Samuel Norman Seaborn from *The West Wing* to me. Please, Aaron Sorkin—REBOOT!

Defining the Roles We Want Our Friends to Play

As an adult, you get to consciously decide what roles are most important to *you*. Warning: Pop culture will *not* give you permission to do this. Do it anyway. In movies and books and on television, friends come in only three varieties: best friends, annoying neighbors, and frenemies. You've likely learned that unless a friendship is *inner circle*, it isn't valuable or worth your time. If you already have a tight-knit group of friends, you may not need or want other varietals. But when you're starting from absolute zero, it's overwhelming to think about the chasm between *no friends* and *soul friends*. What if your friendships didn't *all* need to be deep and intimate? What if . . . drumroll . . . you could have amazing friends whom you adore but do *not* trust?

> *Hang on a sec. How can you have friendship if you don't have trust? Isn't trust the most important thing with friends?*

Not exactly. Hear me out.

I have a dear friend with whom I love to hike. She's a fun "do cool things with" gal pal, but she also happens to be a compulsive liar. I know this. She knows I know. But neither of us cares. We don't have long soulful conversations over coffee, but we climb things and laugh and have a blast together. Because her role is "hiking buddy," I *do* need to trust that she'll navigate the trail and will help me if I take a spill. I *don't* need emotional trust for the friendship to work.

In *Anam Cara: A Book of Celtic Wisdom*, author John O'Donohue writes: "A friend is a loved one who awakens your life in order to free the wild possibilities within you." My hiking buddy pushes me to try new things. She encourages me to literally climb higher and reach farther. She awakens wild possibilities within me. Squishing her into an ill-fitting role (like trusted confidante) would result in a high-conflict dynamic. If I called her out on the inaccuracies in her stories, she'd get defensive and a fight would inevita-

bly ensue. But since I'm clear on who she is and accept the role she's available
to play, our friendship does *not* require love, depth, or vulnerability. Friendships can be fraught with difficulty because the roles we *want* our friends to
play conflict with who they actually are. A conscious awareness of roles en-
ables a powerful shift from resentment to enjoyment. Defining what *trust*
actually means for the specific roles your friends play is important. A generalized "I must trust my friends" ideology is not.

Expectations management and radical acceptance are not the same as
settling for less. In an ideal world, yes, *all* of our friends would be trustwor-
thy, safe, and soulful life companions. In that same ideal world, we'd also
have daily orgasms, zit-free skin, cravings for kale, and dogs who don't pee
on freshly laundered beds. We don't live in that world. Fortunately, when we
toss out idealistic and romanticized notions of friendship, our options dramatically expand. This is true for dating too. Every Level 10 relationship
started as a Level 1. If you don't start with lightweight friends, it's highly
unlikely that heavyweight relationships will spontaneously manifest. If
you're stuck in an isolated friend-free zone, it might be useful to first consider what a "shallow" friendship might look like.

Shallow friends? Really?

Stay with me. Where did we learn that the deep end of the pool is the
only place where good stuff is found? The word *shallow* has a bad reputation.
Shallow people are considered vapid. But shallow water is where you first
learned to swim. Shallow conversations are considered pointless. But just
like small fish and wildlife grow in the shallows, so too do friendships. I love
Lady Gaga's song "Shallow," but deep waters are *not* safe to swim in when
you are first learning a new skill—particularly with friendships and dating.
Things did not fare well for Lady Gaga's Ally and Bradley Cooper's Jack in *A
Star Is Born*, despite the popularity of the Oscar-winning ballad. Shallow
friends are absolutely appropriate as part of the blueprint of your social
world. With clients, I use a fill-in-the-blanks grid to consciously design a
social circle. We start by finding people for the top and bottom and then
strategize ways to fill in the sides.

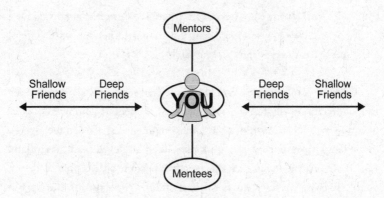

- **Friends (two on each side):** To prevent unhealthy attachment, you need a variety of peers from different parts of your life. One side might represent work friends and the other side might represent parent friends from your kids' school. These relationships can be a mix of deep and shallow. You may *desire* depth but can currently access only shallow people. Give yourself permission to practice your friendship skills and enjoy splashing in the shallow end of the pool. As you build your friendship muscles, your capacity for greater depth will increase.

- **Mentors/Teachers (one or two):** Having people who can pour into *you* helps you avoid burnout and friend fatigue. Find someone who has a quality you admire, has done something you aspire to do, or has the ability to hold space for you without trying to fix you. The nice part about these relationships is you don't have to technically be friends. Therapists, counselors, coaches, and teachers absolutely count.

- **Mentees/Protégés (one or two):** Find someone to whom *you* can be a mentor or teacher, such as a college student, teen, or child. If you're unsure where to start, think about the people you know with kids. If time is a huge factor, remind yourself that this does not require a huge commitment. An annual dinner date with your teenage niece is perfectly acceptable.

The roundtable architecture of this method supports balance. If we are too loaded up on the top section (mentors), we feel disempowered. If we have too many relationships on the bottom (mentees), we can feel overextended and unsupported and are highly likely to develop an overinflated ego. If we just have peers on one side, we become susceptible to dependence. Even if we have peers on both sides, if the top or the bottom section is empty, we miss out on valuable growth opportunities. The pushback I often get is "But, Britt, finding people is way too much work!" My response? *It takes just as much energy to be unhappy alone as it does to construct a social circle.*

You could say that it takes *more* energy to feel unhappy than it does to build relationships, especially when you have carte blanche to toss Instagram-perfect notions of friendship out the window. Remember the Three D's of Friend-Finding. First, redefine what friendship means for you as an adult (*differences*). Then assign the roles in your life-movie cast (*defining*), and the third and final D of the triad is *deconstructing* the top six myths of adult friendships.

Deconstructing the Top Six Myths of Adult Friendships

SIX MYTHS OF ADULT FRIENDSHIPS

1. Good friends give advice.
2. Adult friendships are easy and natural.
3. You need a best friend.

4. You have to invest a lot of time or you're a bad friend.
5. You have to have real-life friends. Social media does not count.
6. Friends are forever.

Myth: Good Friends Give Advice.

I've had many clients disclose that they sought therapy because the therapy room is the one place where they *won't* get advice. While it's natural for friends to share life tips and tricks, it is usually more helpful to *hold space* rather than to *give advice*. Holding space means listening with compassion and without judgment or efforts to fix the other. Skillful space holders ask thoughtful questions but do not presume to know what's best. For therapists, the intention of holding space is to help people access *their* truth rather than trying to sell them on *ours*. Friendships are the same.

Myth: Adult Friendships Are Easy and Natural.

Culture would have you believe adult friendships are as easy as breathing. Nope. *All* relationships—including friendships—take skill, time, and effort to develop and thrive.

Myth: You Need a Best Friend.

This myth takes us back to the differences between friendships in childhood and those in adulthood. Having a bestie is aspirational, but when you are an adult, it is not always possible. Luckily, it is not necessary to have a best friend to reap the full benefits of social connection. To again quote Esther Perel, "Today we turn to one person to provide what an entire village once did: a sense of grounding, meaning, and continuity . . . is it any wonder that so many relationships crumble under the weight of it all?" Though she was talking about romantic relationships in that quote, the sentiment also applies to friendships. You do not need to find your *one and only* bestie.

Myth: You Have to Invest a Lot of Time or You're a Bad Friend.

This myth keeps a lot of wonderful and satisfying connections out of reach. Here's what I call the "We should catch up" cycle of stuck that happens as a result of the time myth—I have a hunch you'll relate:

> *Step 1*: You miss your friend, so you think to call them.
>
> *Step 2*: You want to call them, but then you realize how long it's been since you've called them, and now you feel bad.
>
> *Step 3*: You think you'll need to spend at *least* an hour on the phone with them to make up for how long it's been since you called.
>
> *Step 4*: An hour? Who has a free hour? You don't have a free hour. Forget it. You don't make the call.
>
> *Step 5*: You feel shame.
>
> *Step 6*: Repeat.

This cycle is both unnecessary and easy to fix. As long as you are clear with yourself and your friends about your friendship definition, there's no need to feel shame about not having hours free to catch up. Lilja, my closest friend from college, and I haven't seen each other in years, since we both lead incredibly busy lives. Long gone are the idle hours on picturesque campus benches swapping war stories about guys and stressing about classes. We created what we call the *five-minute catch-up* to circumvent the expectations of hours-long conversations. The five-minute catch-up is exactly what it sounds like. This friendship hack eliminates the pressure to make time, removes the shame of feeling like a bad friend, and sets a structure that accords with our realities. Without these conditions, it is unlikely the friendship would continue to exist.

Myth: You Have to Have Real-Life Friends. Social Media Does Not Count.

Your life, your rules. If social media is a space where you feel connected, seen, validated, and supported, there is no reason to discount your online friends. People can create safe and connected spaces both in person and online. While it is preferable physiologically to be able to hug and connect with people in a three-dimensional space, it is just as valid to have online friends as it is to have real-world friends. Some of my closest friends are people with whom I've never shared physical space.

Myth: Friends Are Forever.

Friends are not always forever. Staying in a relationship out of fear of appearing disloyal is a form of self-betrayal. Outgrowing people and places is a natural part of the life journey. Sometimes the journey means evolving our limits, saying no, or stepping back from a friendship. There is no rule that says you have to keep people in your life just because they've always been there. While it can be sad to leave friendships behind, you are allowed to be both sad and unwilling to remain in an unhealthy relationship.

There are a million friendship concepts that could occupy real estate in these pages. How to set boundaries, how to say no, how to navigate conflict, how to worry about your friends without sacrificing your serenity—these are all useful and important topics. But if we're trying to get out of feeling stuck, we need to walk before we run. *Differentiating* childhood friendships from adulthood friendships, *defining* your friendship roles, and *deconstructing* friendship myths are the linchpins of a flourishing social life. The biggest takeaway I hope you'll pick up from this primer on social connection is said best by friendship expert and author Lydia Denworth: "The science of friendship gives you permission to hang out with your friends and call it healthy."

Now that you've climbed aboard the friends-are-as-important-as-vegetables train, the final section of this chapter focuses on the search for intimacy. If you're currently happy with your romantic relationship, you can skip this section. If you're looking for or struggling with a partner(s), I invite you to pull up a chair for a fireside discussion of relationships that keep us unhappy and stuck. A big disclaimer before we jump in: None of the traditional relationship or dating advice you read here (or anywhere else) applies if the situation includes abuse. Abuse is not a relationship problem. Abuse is not a communication problem. Abuse is not a "maybe if I tried harder" problem. Abuse is an abuser problem, period. Couples therapy is almost *never* recommended when abuse is a factor. If abuse or active addiction is present in your current relationship, the information you need to get unstuck is beyond the scope of this chapter.

Happily Ever After . . . and Other Toxic Fairy Tales

The movie industry should really put a warning label on all romantic comedies. Mythologizing love is a tale as old as time. Belle and the Beast, Edward and Bella, Sandy and Danny, Jack and Rose, Romeo and Juliet—it's often the movie couples we idolize the most that provide the best examples of what *not* to do in a relationship. The science and psychology of dating tell a very different story about our favorite fictional couples:

Swoon-Worthy Movie Couple	Toxic Relationship Dynamics
Belle and the Beast (*Beauty and the Beast*)	Stockholm syndrome (bonding with your abuser), love addiction, emotional abuse, physical abuse, isolation, coercion, narcissism
Edward and Bella (*Twilight*)	Stalking, emotional abuse, threats, physical abuse, isolation

Swoon-Worthy Movie Couple	Toxic Relationship Dynamics
Sandy and Danny (*Grease*)	Emotional abuse, changing who you are to please your partner, gaslighting, cheating, lying, date rape
Jack and Rose	Love bombing, emotional abuse, boundary issues, the relationship lasted only two days, idealization, obsession
Romeo and Juliet	Emotional abuse, boundary issues, stalking, terrible communication skills, the relationship lasted only five days

Before you accuse me of being a romance buzzkill, consider the science of dating.

A volcano of brain chemicals erupts when people connect. The flood of adrenaline, dopamine, and serotonin torpedoes our sense of logic. The result? We surf the roaring white-water rapids of new-relationship brain and ignore things like eating, sleeping, and seeing friends. While this is *not* sustainable, the hormone high is a normal (and fun) part of the courtship process. It takes roughly a year to recalibrate and come down off "couple cocaine" brain chemistry to the point where perception and judgment return. Attempting to prolong the hormone-high phase is like regularly consuming mass quantities of sugar—eventually you start to feel sick. Avoiding the perils and pitfalls of dating requires knowledge of the toxic fairy tales that keep us *all* stuck:

- All you need is love.
- Don't go to sleep angry.
- Monogamy is your only option.
- You should spend every waking moment with your person.
- You need someone to complete you.

All You Need Is Love.

It is possible to deeply and profoundly love someone and still not have the relationship work. While love may indeed conquer all in the spiritual sense, in the physical human form as we experience it, love's power is finite. If love's power were infinite, the love of a mother would always heal her child, the love of a spouse would always cure dementia, and the love of a friend would always triumph over addiction. The presence of love does not guarantee a happily ever after. Understanding and accepting human limitations, removing ourselves from unhealthy situations, and staying committed to reality keep us healthy as we navigate our romantic relationships. You can be in a relationship only with a person, not with potential. Believing in someone's potential is a compassionate and beautiful gift—as long as it doesn't come at the expense of your own emotional and physical safety. Once, in the aftermath of a relationship explosion, I sat on a dimly lit street with my good friend Jenn. I was chain-smoking Marlboros as quickly as I could inhale. "But I *love* him!" I sobbed. "Honey," she said calmly, "I know you do. And that will *never* be enough to make him change."

> You can be in a relationship only with a person, not with potential.

Don't Go to Sleep Angry.

This is an age-old piece of advice that is in direct conflict with neuroscience. Have you ever tried to have a rational conversation about *anything* while you were sleep-deprived? It's difficult. Have you ever tried to have a rational conversation while you're sleep-deprived *and* angry? Disaster. Rather than forcing yourself to slug things out for hours, making a mature and respectful decision to take time and space to rest can help prevent minor tussles from turning nuclear.

Monogamy Is Your Only Option.

There are as many expressions of healthy relationships as there are people *in* relationships. Monogamy is one option. Open relationships, swinging, monogamish, polyamory—all of these are also viable options. In *More Than Two*, author Franklin Veaux writes: "Polyamory can feel threatening because it upsets our fairy-tale assumption that the right partner will keep us safe from change . . . the fairy tale tells us that with the right partner, happiness just happens. But happiness is something we re-create every day. And it comes more from our outlook than from the things around us." I've seen profound shifts in clients who consciously shift from monogamy into a lifestyle that better reflects their genuine needs and desires. Consensual non-monogamy is not a hedonic hall pass. All iterations of non-monogamy require advanced communication skills, thoughtfulness, and consideration. Though monogamy is a perfectly valid choice, if it is based on a fantasy ideal, the relationship becomes a fertile ground for cheating.

You Should Spend Every Waking Moment with Your Person.

If you try to build a campfire with the logs too close together, the fire fizzles out. Space and oxygen are required for flames to burn. New relationships are the same. Too much togetherness increases the odds that the relationship will collapse under the pressure. I've had both friends and clients look at me like I'm crazy when I suggest that one to two times alone per week is more than enough time to cultivate a new relationship. "*What?!* That's not enough! I want to see my partner more than that!" While I totally get that sentiment, all relationships need space to thrive.

It's tempting to think that finding a significant other is an express ticket to happily ever after. If pair bonding provided the skeleton key to bliss, we would not see such abysmal divorce statistics. Finding a partner is the cherry on a full life—not the source of life itself. While it may be tempting to blow off friends, family, and interests to burrow into a "couple cave," remember from earlier in the chapter that an active social life supports health and growth. If you do not first cultivate a solid base of friends, interests, and self-care routines, approach romantic relationships with extreme caution. You know the phrase *It takes a village to raise a child*? I'd also say that *It takes a village to raise a relationship*.

You Need Someone to Complete You.

We are taught from early childhood to look for someone to complete us, to save us, and to make us whole. Women are trained to be damsels in distress searching for white knights. We are trained to believe that we are not enough. We are trained to believe that without a romantic partner we will end up morphing into crazy cat ladies.

NO.

When you approach dating from a deficit mindset (the belief that you're missing something), the likelihood you'll end up in an unhealthy relationship is high. Why? Because "deficit dating" leads to unhealthy attachments and a toxic dynamic I call *projection bonding*.

Projection bonding is the thing that happens when you are attracted to qualities in other people you *desire* but think you *lack*. If you feel disempowered, you'll be drawn toward powerful people. If you believe you lack creativity, you'll be drawn to artists. The wild truth is that you already possess everything you need—despite what *appears* to be all evidence to the contrary. *Everyone* has creative capacity. *Everyone* has an inner genius. Until we integrate our lost shadow parts (see chapter 4), we will continue to find them in other people and confuse *projection* with *attraction*. Projection bonds cement us in unhealthy relationships and create terror at the idea of leaving because to leave *them* would be to leave *ourselves*. When we form a projection bond with another, we compromise ourselves in damaging ways to preserve the relationship. Projection bonds gain power from the belief that we lack qualities like beauty, talent, spirituality, leadership, or intelligence. We remain in relationships even if they annihilate our sanity.

Conclusion: The Three D's of Dating

Remember the Three D's of Friend-Finding? With a few minor modifications, you can apply the same principles to your dating life:

1. *Differentiating* between movie relationships and real relationships
2. *Defining* the roles we want our partners to play
3. *Deconstructing* toxic fairy tales that keep us stuck

And a reminder—there are *no* "mixed signals" when it comes to dating. If someone is *interested* and *available*, they will not play games. If someone is *not* interested and *not* available, you'll know quickly. If someone is interested but is *not* available emotionally, you'll feel confusion and unease. Interested + unavailable = mixed signal. A mixed signal from *them* is a clear signal for *you* to pass. Interested + unavailable is where you'll ride most of the relational roller coasters of the dating world.

Using the Three D's brings priceless clarity and focus to your adventures in human-ing. When you *differentiate* between movie romance and reality, when you *define* the roles you want your partner to play, and when you *deconstruct* toxic fairy-tale myths, you save a ton of time when you eliminate mismatches. Buying into the cultural myths about friendships and dating is like drinking bleach to cure a viral infection: it doesn't work, it isn't based on science, and it is extremely dangerous for your health.

Bottom-Line Takeaways

1. Not having friends can have the same impact on your health as smoking cigarettes.
2. You don't need to have a best friend.
3. Unconditional trust is not a realistic (or necessary) goal for adult relationships.

4. Consider the roles you want your friends to play—then choose accordingly.
5. Don't try to box your friends into ill-fitting roles.
6. Social media friends count as friends if you want them to count as friends.
7. Most movie and TV couples—even our favorites—are toxic.
8. It is *not* healthy to spend every waking moment with your partner.
9. Sometimes love isn't enough to sustain a relationship.
10. It takes roughly a year before your brain comes down off of "couple cocaine" brain chemistry.

Dos and Don'ts:

Do	Don't
Look through your contacts and see if there are any people with whom you can reconnect.	Try to find a bestie. Shallow friendships are fine when you're starting out.
Get honest with yourself about the types of friends you actually want versus the types of friends you think you should have.	Betray yourself by attending events you'd rather avoid to spend time with people you don't like.
Take time to think about what you value in a romantic relationship.	Think you need to have a relationship that looks like someone else's. Do what makes the most sense for your unique situation.
Give yourself permission to have time boundaries with friends and romantic partners.	Force yourself to spend every waking moment with a friend or partner—relationships need space to thrive.

FIVE-MINUTE CHALLENGES

1. Write a permission slip to yourself that says "I give myself permission to _____ [say no to weddings, minimize time, not stay on the phone for hours, etc.] in my friendships."

2. The role I most need my friends to play right now in my life is _____ [advice giver/confidante/do-things-with buddy/listener/bringer of food/child-watcher/etc.].

3. Take the friendship matrix from page 123, copy it into a notebook, and fill it in to whatever degree you can.

4. If you have any blank spaces on the grid, think of one or two ways you can find people to fill in the gaps.

CHAPTER 7

The Emotionally Unskilled Family

> I think a dysfunctional family is any family with more than one person in it.
>
> —Mary Karr

When you think of the healthiest, happiest, most high-functioning fictional families, who comes to mind? Danny Tanner and his earnest heart-to-hearts on *Full House*? Uncle Phil and his stern but supportive pep talks on *The Fresh Prince of Bel-Air*? The Rose family and their never-give-up attitude on *Schitt's Creek*? The flawed yet lovable Belchers on *Bob's Burgers*?

Nah.

The healthiest, happiest, and most high-functioning fictional family of all time is—wait for it—the Addams Family.*

While *The Addams Family* appears at first glance to be a show filled with gloom and doom, misery, and "who the hell are these people?" madness, a closer look reveals a different story. Consider the facts:

- Morticia and Gomez enjoy a strong marriage with passionate sex. Lots of it.

---

*Fun fact: The motto of the Addams Family is *Sic Gorgiamus Allos Subjectatos Nunc*, or "We Gladly Feast on Those Who Would Subdue Us." Love the sentiment, though I think the translation of the Latin might be incorrect.

▸ The family places a high value on unique self-expression.
▸ Morticia and Gomez each have their own interests, hobbies, and social supports.
▸ Outsiders are welcomed into the family.
▸ There is never yelling, hitting, or abuse . . . without consent.
▸ They are a multigenerational family living harmoniously under one roof.

Addams family hobbies are not safe to try at home—playing with electric chairs and drinking cyanide will kill you. But Addams family *dynamics* are straight out of the "this is what a healthy family looks like" textbook. I've seen the damage inflicted by toxic families. Narcissistic mothers. Absent fathers. Sexually abusive relatives. Domestic violence. Drug addiction. As someone from a dysfunctional family, I could set up camp in the "my family is crazy" section of the bookstore for years.

But what if you *don't* identify as a childhood abuse survivor?

If your family generally sailed along without capsizing, you may feel guilty for having *any* complaints. You may come from a family that isn't overtly abusive; your family may have had plenty of food and no worries about the electricity bill. And yet you still sometimes feel hurt. You still sometimes feel anger, pain, or sadness about cutting words or thoughtless actions. If you have a healthy-ish family, you've likely tucked your pain away and feel guilty for feeling it at all. You may feel shame and think, *My family life was pretty good, so why do I feel so bad?* or *I don't come from a dysfunctional family—so what is my problem?*

This chapter is for you.

We *all* come from dysfunctional families. "Dysfunctional family" is not a category—it's a *continuum*. If you come from a highly toxic and abusive family—I see you. The information in this chapter is primarily geared toward relatively functional families, but the information can still be applicable to any situation. *Every* family falls somewhere on the continuum of dysfunction. If you're the product of an egg and sperm collision, you'll inevitably sustain emotional injuries from your family. Why? All human families are made up of people, and people aren't perfect. In *Love Is Not Enough*, David W. Earle writes: "Wounded parents often unintentionally inflict pain and suffering on their children and these childhood wounds cause a laundry list of maladaptive behaviors." Unintentionally created pain is still pain. You have a right to your feelings.

"Normal" Families Also Cause Trauma

Twelve-Step program participants use the expression "Normal is just a setting on your washing machine." There really isn't such a thing as a normal family. For the purposes of this chapter, we'll use the word *normal* to describe families with a general absence of high-level dysfunction such as abuse or unsafe environmental conditions.

In my practice, I consistently hear people from so-called normal families say:

- ▸ "Other people had it so much worse."
- ▸ "It's not like I was abused."
- ▸ "It's stupid for me to be upset—I had a great childhood."
- ▸ "I feel bad for getting triggered by my mom—she did an amazing job raising me."
- ▸ "My dad means well—I really shouldn't be bothered by what he says."

I've said this before and I'll say it again—perspective is healthy; comparison is not. You are not crazy for feeling anger, pain, and sadness about your family. *All* families cause emotional wounds. Chapter 3 defined *trauma* as brain indigestion. Another definition comes from the Meadows of Wickenburg, a residential treatment facility in Arizona and the mothership for all things related to trauma, addiction, and mental health. The Meadows defines trauma as "anything less than nurturing." If trauma can be caused by anything less than nurturing, we all experience it (to a degree) and we all cause it (to a degree). Parents often tell me, "I'm afraid I'm going to mess up my kids." My response? "You don't have to be afraid that you 'might' mess up your kids. You're one hundred percent guaranteed to mess up your kids."

Really?

You're 100 percent guaranteed to mess up your kids because you're *100 percent human*. But you don't have to beat yourself up for making mistakes and messing up. As someone who is child-free by choice, I don't speak the language of parenting. But as a trained play therapist I'm fluent in the language of children. I can attest that mess-ups (unintentional mistakes) do *not* mess up kids. What messes up kids are intentionally inflicted injuries, parents who refuse to address their mess-ups when they mess up, and environmental factors outside parental control. My friend and colleague Vanessa Cornell, mother of five and founder of NUSHU, a women's healing collective, says, "I'm proud to be an imperfect child of imperfect parents. And an imperfect mom to imperfect kids." Your kids don't need perfect parents. They need *human* parents who will teach them how to be imperfectly human too.

In *The Five People You Meet in Heaven*, Mitch Albom writes: "All parents damage their children. It cannot be helped. Youth, like pristine glass, absorbs the prints of its handlers. Some parents smudge, others crack, a few shatter childhoods completely into jagged little pieces." The point of parenting is not perfection. Healthy parents don't *avoid* mistakes—they *identify* and do their best to *correct* mistakes. Remind yourself that this chapter is neither an attack on your parents nor a critique of your parenting. Unless there's abuse, most families don't fall neatly into categories of good and bad. Instead, we'll use the terms *emotionally skilled* and *emotionally unskilled*.

What Is a Family?

For the purposes of this chapter, *family* is defined as the people with whom you spent the majority of your time from birth to age sixteen.* This includes parents, extended family, nannies, neighbors, and anyone in your home who was in charge of your care. The information here does not require you to blame anyone. You don't have to cut off contact with your brother or confront your mother. You may be quick to write off low-level emotional wounds by thinking, *It wasn't that bad . . . other people have it so much worse.* But over time, even low-level emotional wounds can have an effect on your sense of worth and well-being. You don't squint at your computer screen and think, *Well, other people have worse problems with their eyes, so I don't deserve to go to the optometrist.* You have a right to feel and to heal your emotional pain—even if your family is amazing.

A Very Brief Overview of Attachment and Parenting

There are mountains of textbooks and articles about parenting and attachment. To get unstuck, you don't need to read all that material, but it helps to have a working understanding of parenting approaches and attachment styles so you can know what was *supposed* to happen. Don't panic if your family lands on one of the less-than-ideal categories. You don't have to call your parents and shout, "You screwed me up with your parenting approach, and *that's* why I have intimacy issues!" Once again, this information is *not* to

---

* Many cultures define families differently. The definition used here is not the only definition, but since this is only one chapter's worth of info, I chose to limit the scope of the discussion.

blame your parents or to shame your parenting. Maya Angelou wrote: "I did then what I knew how to do. Now that I know better, I do better." Identifying gaps in your family's skill set allows you to do better and to get unstuck. As David W. Earle put it, "many of the habits of dysfunctional families are not from the lack of love but are the result of fear. Knowing the love-limiting habits and behaviors of dysfunctional families is a wonderful beginning to lower the fear, allowing us to be real, allowing us all to learn how to love better."

The following section provides you with a very brief overview and includes examples from fictional families. In the 1950s, Drs. John Bowlby and Mary Ainsworth outlined four primary attachment styles, and in the 1960s Dr. Diana Baumrind described four primary parenting approaches.

ATTACHMENT STYLES

Attachment Style	Definition	Fictional Example
Secure Attachment	Securely attached children trust they are loved, cared for, and safe. They are happy to play and explore alone and also happy to interact with other people.	Wednesday and Pugsley from *The Addams Family*. They play together and alone, they get along with the other adults in the family, and they pursue their interests with curiosity and openness.
Avoidant Attachment	Children with avoidant attachment are wary of other humans. They do not trust people and prefer to play alone. Avoidant children may sometimes be mislabeled "independent."	Lydia Deetz from *Beetlejuice*. She's a loner, she avoids interactions with her family, and she prefers the company of dead people. She says things like, "My whole life is a dark room. One big dark room."

ATTACHMENT STYLES

Attachment Style	Definition	Fictional Example
Ambivalent Attachment	These children are anxious, insecure, and often clingy. They vacillate between wanting attention/affection and rejecting attention/affection.	Kevin McCallister from *Home Alone*. He claims to hate his family and initially wants them to disappear, but it's also clear that he cares about his family and wants to be loved and accepted by them.
Disorganized Attachment	These children display extreme emotional explosions, complete emotional numbness, and everything in between.	Anakin Skywalker from the Star Wars universe. He started out as a sweet child, but the absence of a father and the murder of his mother created intense attachment trauma. Anakin's relationships with his wife and mentors were turbulent. He eventually turned to the dark side and became Darth Vader.*
		* Not all children with disorganized attachment grow up to be Darth Vader. Children with this attachment style are often stigmatized. Disorganized attachment is often mislabeled as an *internal* sickness rather than an *attachment* challenge.

PARENTING APPROACHES

Parenting Approach	Definition	Fictional Example
Authoritarian	These parents demand obedience and respect. They set rigid rules and enact strict consequences. Their discipline style is punishing rather than problem-solving.	Miss Hannigan from *Annie*. She regularly doles out emotional and physical abuse to the girls in the orphanage.
Authoritative	These parents set limits and enforce consequences, but do so from a place of compassion and validation. They value the child's input. Authoritative parents stay calm when they enforce rules and do not punish from a place of anger.	Elastigirl, a.k.a. Helen Parr, a.k.a. Mrs. Incredible from *The Incredibles*. She is involved with the children and sets limits and rules, but she does not threaten. She explains why things are the way they are, and she's warm and responsive to the children. She owns her errors, as demonstrated when she tells her daughter Violet, "It isn't your fault. It wasn't fair for me to suddenly ask so much of you."
Permissive	These parents are present but uninvolved. There are no rules and no consequences. As one of the characters in Frances Hodgson Burnett's novel *The Secret Garden* puts it: "Th' two worst things as can happen to a child is never to have his own way—or always to have it."	Veruca Salt's father in *Willy Wonka & the Chocolate Factory*. No further explanation needed.

PARENTING APPROACHES

Parenting Approach	Definition	Fictional Example
Neglectful	These parents tend to ignore or abandon their children. Neglectful parents aren't always malicious, but they remain uninvolved and uninterested in participating in their children's lives.	Winifred Banks, the mother in the original *Mary Poppins* movie, is a good example of a neglectful parent. Although she was kind and loving, Mrs. Banks ultimately displayed a lack of interest in the children and was quick to pawn them off on their string of nannies.

If you started to zone out reading these charts, you can catch up by looking at the images below.

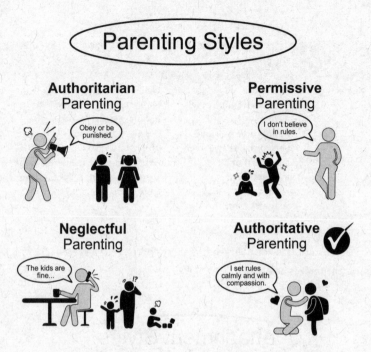

In an emotionally skilled family, the kids (generally) demonstrate secure attachment and the parents (generally) use an authoritative parenting style. The acronym SKILLED is an easy way to remember the elements of a healthy family system.

Healthy Families Are SKILLED

- ▸ Seek solutions.
- ▸ Keep communication direct.
- ▸ Invite open dialogue.
- ▸ Listen to one another.
- ▸ Learn from one another.

▸ **E**mpathize with one another.
▸ **D**isagree respectfully.

Families who consistently nail all of the SKILLED elements *still* create wounds. Even though there is no *intention* to cause harm, some family members (especially older parents who are set in their ways) scoff at the idea that they need to upgrade their skills. In *Bradshaw On: The Family*, author John Bradshaw observes: "Perhaps nothing so accurately characterizes dysfunctional families as denial. The denial forces members to keep believing the myths and vital lies in spite of the facts, or to keep expecting that the same behaviors will have different outcomes." If you're ready to dissolve denial, the next section illustrates ten unskillful family dynamics. I use the word *unskillful* to describe families who operate at a normal level of dysfunction. If physical, emotional, or sexual harm was part of your childhood experience, that is *not* an unskillful dynamic—that is abuse.*

---

*The ten dynamics described here also are present in abusive families, but to a much higher degree, and they are often done intentionally to cause harm.

Ten Signs of an Emotionally Unskilled Family

1. Non-Malicious Gaslighting

Gaslighting is when someone causes you to doubt your perception of reality. The term comes from the 1944 Alfred Hitchcock psychological thriller *Gaslight*. In the film, Ingrid Bergman's character sees lights flicker and hears strange noises. When she asks her husband to confirm her perceptions, he tells her she's going crazy and that it's all in her head. But she's not crazy—her husband wants her money and intentionally manipulates the environment so she'll lose her mind and get locked away in an institution. Gaslighting is usually associated with narcissism and high-level abuse, but even healthy people from healthy families participate in *non-malicious gaslighting*.

What's an example of non-malicious gaslighting? Imagine a mom who comes home from work stressed, overwhelmed, and frustrated. Her little daughter asks, "Mommy, what's wrong?" The mom replies, "Nothing, honey. Everything is fine. Mommy is fine." This parent is gaslighting even though the *intent* is not malicious. How is this gaslighting? The child accurately picks up on her mom's distress cues—she intuitively knows Mom is not "fine." But when the mom says nothing is wrong, the daughter learns to doubt her own perceptions.

A more skillful way for this parent to handle the situation would be to say, "You're seeing that Mommy is upset. You're right. I am upset, but you don't have to worry. I will be okay. I'm not upset with you and there's nothing you need to do." Gaslighting creates serious injuries over time. Chronic gaslighting—even if it's done with non-malicious intent—can create the same consequences as those experienced by survivors of abusive gaslighting. Being frequently gaslit as a child can cause indecisiveness, shaky self-confidence, and an unstable sense of self as an adult.

What to Do About Gaslighting: Confrontation is *not* typically recommended for gaslighting, since the person doing the gaslighting may be quick to deny, minimize, or further invalidate your feelings. Instead, call on an emotionally skillful friend (or therapist) and ask them for feedback. This is called reality testing. Families with non-malicious gaslighting tend to experience high levels of anxiety. If this is you, chapter 1 covers anxiety management strategies.

2. Parentification

It should *not* be the job of kids to take care of parents who have the capacity to take care of themselves. With parentification, children are responsible for the tasks of parenting and/or the management of their parents' feelings. If you've ever worried about making your parents angry or upset, you've experienced parentification. Skillful parents manage their own feelings and do not rely on their children to tap-dance around triggers. Kimberlee Roth writes: "Parentified children learn to take responsibility for themselves and others early on. They tend to fade into the woodwork and let others take center stage. . . . They may have difficulty accepting care and attention." Healthy parents manage their *own* needs and do not demand care from or intimacy with their children. In *Voices in the Family*, Daniel Gottlieb writes: "More often than not, it's disrespectful to them (our children)—and disrespectful to their struggle with their tasks in life—if our own anxiety as parents makes us cling to our children. It's disrespectful if we demand more intimacy than they are willing or able to give."

What to Do About Parentification: When you worry that your choices will upset your parents, remind yourself that *they* are responsible for managing their feelings. When your family invites you on a guilt trip, feel free to RSVP with *"Sorry, unable to attend."* This is easier said than done. You'll find boundary scripts in chapter 5 to help you when confrontation is necessary.

3. Infantilization

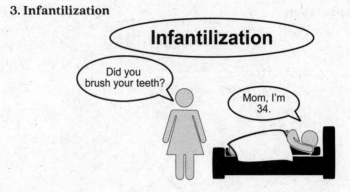

The reverse of parentification is infantilization. This is when parents try to keep children small and dependent because it makes the parent feel needed. Infantilization can happen at any age and is particularly noticeable during the holidays. Novelist V. C. Andrews writes: "I believe, though I'm not sure, once you are an adult, and come back to the home of your parents to live, for some odd reason, you're reduced to being a child again, and dependent."

What to Do About Infantilization: Remember that you are a fully grown and capable adult. If you don't feel like a fully grown and capable adult, we'll cover how to get unstuck in chapter 9.

4. Triangulation

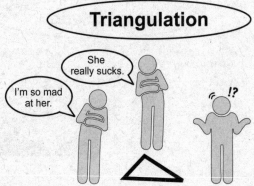

Triangulation is when two people talk about a third person without that third person being present; this behavior can carve deep cuts into your sense of well-being. In *Nonviolent Communication*, Marshall B. Rosenberg writes, "While we may not consider the way we talk to be 'violent,' words often lead to hurt and pain, whether for others or ourselves." This may look like your mother and aunt gossiping about your weight. Or it could look like your sister and your father whispering about your divorce.

What to Do About Triangulation: The solution to family triangles is to create direct lines of communication. You can refuse to participate in triangulation dynamics and request that your family stop triangulating. A caution about requests: Remember, requests require someone *else* to do something you want them to do. You can ask, you can beg, you can yell, pout, and stomp—but you cannot control someone else's choices. What you *can* do is set boundaries. Boundaries are what *you* choose to do in response to someone *else's* choices. You are in control with boundaries. If your family won't stop triangulating, stronger boundaries may be necessary.

5. Perfectionism

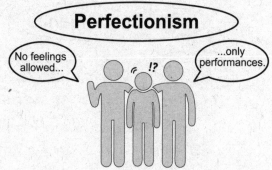

Striving toward *excellence* produces joy. Striving toward *perfection* produces shame. Striving for excellence is an achievable dream. Striving for perfection is an impossible dream. Perfectionism is not a virtue—it is a form of emotional self-harm. Elizabeth Gilbert writes: "Perfectionism is just fear in fancy shoes and a mink coat." You could also think of perfectionism as self-hatred dressed in diamonds.

What to Do About Perfectionism: If you come from a perfectionistic family, getting unstuck requires you to create your own set of values. Brené Brown taught us that empathy is the antidote to shame. Similarly, authenticity is the antidote to perfection. Find people with whom you can be your beautifully messy, flawed, imperfect self. Those are your people.

> Authenticity is the antidote to perfection.

6. Productionism

Thought leaders, scientists, and psychologists all agree that play is an essential component of healthy childhood development. Swiss psychologist Jean Piaget said, "If you want to be creative, stay in part a child, with the creativity and invention that characterizes children before they are deformed by adult society." Kay Redfield Jamison writes: "Children need the freedom and time to play. Play is not a luxury. Play is a necessity."

There are stacks of scientific studies that validate play's importance for learning, bonding, fostering creativity, reducing stress, developing the brain, improving social skills, processing feelings, and building language skills. Yet many emotionally unskilled families view play as a frivolous waste of time. These families suffer from what I call productionism. If perfectionism is a compulsive need to be perfect, productionism is a compulsive need to produce. Since families with productionism prioritize productivity over fun, they often struggle to play, sing, dance, and create.

What to Do About Productionism: If play wasn't valued in your family, you may struggle with spontaneity or creativity or may find it hard to experience sexual pleasure as an adult. The single most useful resource I've ever seen for recovering from productionism is Julia Cameron's classic, *The Artist's Way*.

7. Blurred Lines

The term *blurred lines* is used to reflect a dynamic in which the boundaries of the body are not taught or respected. Children with strong body boundaries know their body belongs to *them*. Children with blurred body boundaries are taught to accept inappropriate comments and unwanted physical contact without complaint. An example would be a father who looks at his teenage daughter and says, "Wow, kid. Look at those biceps. You should give your mother some workout tips." Or a child who is told, "Be nice to your grandmother and give her a hug." This dynamic is problematic. Why? Receiving comments (even positive ones) about your body and being told to give or receive hugs (even if you don't want them) sends the message that your body doesn't belong to you. If you've ever said things like this—no shame. Most parents genuinely want to do right by their kids, and it's only when we have more information that we can make different choices. Other examples of blurred lines include:

- ► Being forced to give a parent back or foot rubs
- ► Not having locks or privacy in the bathroom
- ► Being forced to give hugs
- ► Being tickled without consent

The blurred lines dynamic occurs on a continuum. Families with the occasional lapse in boundaries fall on the lower end. At the higher end of the continuum is a dynamic referred to in the clinical world as *emotional incest*, a term coined by Dr. Kenneth Adams in the 1980s. Although this term makes us uncomfortable, such a dynamic happens often enough and is damaging enough to merit such extreme language. Author Robert Burney writes: "One of the most pervasive, traumatic, and damaging dynamics that occurs in families . . . is emotional incest. It is rampant in our society but there is still very little written or discussed about it." Because emotional incest is not overtly violent or sexual, it often goes undetected.*

The impact of blurred lines can be devastating, especially because it often doesn't look like anything is wrong.† Adult children who experienced the extreme end of the blurred lines continuum often manifest the same symptoms as children who have experienced physical sexual abuse. Disclaimer: I am *not* equating emotional sexual abuse with physical sexual abuse. However, the symptomology that presents with both is strikingly similar.

What to Do About Blurred Lines: The first step in changing a pattern is to recognize its presence. Consider your relationships with parents and caregivers and honestly ask yourself if there were any blurry interactions. Reassure yourself you are *not* crazy. Rather than write it off as "just Dad being Dad," remind yourself that blurred lines—even if that dynamic was "normal" in your family—can be a very real problem. One of the most common consequences of blurred lines as a child is a compulsive relationship with food or chemicals as an adult. If this is you, chapter 8 can give you tools and information to get you unstuck.

---

*The literature on emotional incest includes other issues besides body boundaries. Those discussions go beyond the scope of this chapter.

†The dynamic of blurred lines refers to well-meaning and mostly functional families who *sincerely* didn't know that these behaviors cause harm. If your family is toxic or dysfunctional, blurred lines land squarely under the category of abuse.

8. Controlling

Controlling families use intimidation, guilt, and emotional outbursts to maintain power over relationships, finances, chores, etc. Yelling is one method of control, although not all controlling people yell (and not all yelling is controlling). Controlling family dynamics fall under the category of verbal abuse. In *The Tao of Fully Feeling*, Pete Walker writes:

> Verbal abuse is the use of language to shame, scare or hurt another. Dysfunctional parents routinely use name-calling, sarcasm, and destructive criticism to overpower and control their children. Verbal abuse is as commonplace in the American family as homework and table manners. It is modeled as socially acceptable in almost every sitcom on television.

What to Do About Controlling Family Members: If you have a history of tolerating controlling behavior from unskillful family members, it can be helpful to ask yourself what you fear will happen if you *don't* comply. If family members refuse to upgrade their skills, you may need to shift your energy to relationships outside the family system. The exercises in chapter 6 can help you cultivate emotionally skillful friendships. In the words of Dr. Wayne W. Dyer, "Friends are God's way of apologizing for your family."

9. Closed System

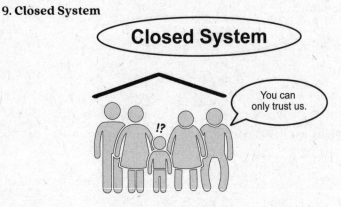

Emotionally unskillful family systems are often closed systems. This means that outside people are not trusted, outside influences are not permitted, conformity is mandated, and the system is resistant to change of any kind— even healthy change. Commonly heard mantras in a closed family system include:

- Because I said so, that's why.
- Do as I say, not as I do.
- You can't trust anyone outside this family.
- This is the way things have always been done.
- Don't air your dirty laundry.
- What happens in this house stays in this house.

In contrast, an *open* family system welcomes communication, is willing to receive new information, and is open to change. Open family systems welcome new perspectives and adapt accordingly. They recognize the value of outside input and are flexible rather than rigid. As Virginia Satir put it, "feelings of worth can flourish only in an atmosphere where individual differences are appreciated, mistakes are tolerated, communication is open, and rules are flexible—the kind of atmosphere that is found in a nurturing family."

What to Do About a Closed Family System: It is unlikely you'll be able to convince your family of origin to shift from closed to open. Instead, focus on the people in your life who *are* willing to receive updated information, to make changes when necessary, and to stay open-minded to new ways of being, thinking, and doing.

10. Rigid Roles

Emotionally skillful families are open to change and growth. Emotionally unskillful families assign specific roles to their members, and any attempt to change roles is met with resistance. If you were thought of as the smart one in your family, you may have been discouraged to try out for soccer. If you were labeled as the athletic one, your interest in joining debate club or auditioning for the school musical may have been mocked.

Rigid role dynamics are often quite pronounced in families with addiction. Even though family members consciously want their addicted loved one to recover, *unconscious* resistance often develops. The classic example of this pattern is enabling. Terry Ciszek writes: "Without getting help, the enabler will work to minimize the consequences of the addict's actions to keep the family on course. And the addict will have little motivation to get help for the addiction." Why would a family resist the recovery process? Recovery demands authenticity, truth-telling, and change. When someone with an addiction recovers, long-repressed family secrets often emerge. You can't change one part of a family system without creating change for everyone. The shift from addict to truth teller comes at a price—many families struggle to grow beyond their comfortable and familiar roles.

What to Do About Rigid Roles: You can't force your family to change any more than you can force someone with an addiction to recover. According to the Three C's of Al-Anon, a support program for families and friends of alcoholics, you didn't *cause* the addiction, you can't *control* it, and you can't *cure* it. If your family tries to put you in a box, you may need to take a step back and focus on relationships where change and growth are encouraged. My friend and colleague Nate Postlethwait says, "If you were born into a family that had expectations for you to play a specific role in order for them to affirm you, your work is deconstructing their ideas of who you were supposed to be and demanding respect for who you are. You do not owe your family a character."

My Family Is Emotionally Unskilled. Now What?

If you've made it this far, congratulations. It takes courage to honestly assess your family's skill level and to break through denial. The first step in the change process is to acknowledge a pattern's presence. Check. What's next? The next step is to practice mindful *responding* rather than automatic *reacting*. Your first impulse will be to do what you've always done. Don't feel bad if your first impulse is to react unskillfully. That impulse is like the first pancake of a batch—gooey, misshapen, burnt, and usually inedible. No one feels guilty about tossing the first pancake—it's expected. Your *second* impulse is where the habit gets broken—where you *respond* rather than *react*. Your second impulse is the second pancake. Pia Mellody writes: "We must learn to do the things our dysfunctional parents did not teach us to do: appropriately esteem ourselves, set functional boundaries, be aware of and acknowledge our reality, take care of our adult needs and wants, and experience our reality moderately." How? The acronym BUILD is a quick way to remember your menu of options when faced with unskillful family dynamics:

Boundaries. Emotional health *cannot* exist without boundaries.
   Boundary expert Nedra Tawwab writes: "Your wellness hinges on your boundaries." This is true for your individual wellness as well as your family's emotional skillfulness.

Unsubscribe from "I should" and "I have to." These phrases are based on obligation and keep you stuck in patterns. Instead, use *choice*-based phrases like "I could" and "I choose to."

Investigate your perceptions by reality testing.

Label your *own* thoughts and feelings so you're clear on where you stand.

Delay compassion and forgiveness until you've *fully* acknowledged your injuries.

Compassion is healthy *if and only if* its presence coincides with boundaries. Boundaries without compassion can feel rigid and unkind, but compassion without boundaries is codependence. Compassion without boundaries is self-betrayal at best and self-harm at worst. Remember that compassion and boundaries are *not* mutually exclusive. What about forgiveness? You may want to jump over your emotional injuries in a rush to get to forgiveness. Here are three key things to know about forgiveness:

> Compassion without boundaries is self-betrayal at best and self-harm at worst.

1. Forgiveness is a beautiful spiritual ideal, but it is *not* required to heal trauma.

2. When you jump over your wounds in a rush to forgive, you minimize and invalidate your reality. This is self-inflicted gaslighting.

3. Forgiveness is often an overflow of emotional healing—but it is *not* a *prerequisite* to emotional healing. You do not have to forgive if you don't want to forgive.

Conclusion

Family patterns are often passed down through generations and can be incredibly difficult to change. You'll likely experience a mix of anger, grief, pain, guilt, and sadness as you take an honest inventory of your family's skill set.* The work is uncomfortable, but the rewards are undeniable. In the Twelve-Step bible for recovering addicts, *The Big Book of Alcoholics Anonymous*, there is a section called "The Promises." This is a list of rewards you can count on if you commit to the work of change. These promises are applicable to anyone in the process of getting unstuck from *anything*—including family dynamics. The promises include:

> ▸ We are going to know a new freedom and a new happiness.
> ▸ We will not regret the past nor wish to shut the door on it.
> ▸ We will intuitively know how to handle situations which used to baffle us.
> ▸ If we are painstaking about this phase of our development, we will be amazed before we are halfway through.

When you want to quit, remind yourself that the alternative is to stay stuck. In the presence of willingness, access to resources, and accurate information, miraculous shifts *can* and *do* happen. No matter how skillful or unskillful your family of origin, it is never too late for *you* to change. When you commit to staying on the path even when it's muddy and steep, you'll eventually find yourself doing things that used to feel impossible. Triggers that would have spiraled you into overwhelm will suddenly become manageable. You'll find yourself experiencing anger and sadness without your anger and sadness taking over. You'll be able to set boundaries without guilt and

---

*Chapter 9, "Becoming An Emotional Adult," walks you through the grieving process.

shame, and you'll feel empowered to chart your course in whatever direction you choose.

All of these promises apply to you. You can do this.

BOTTOM-LINE TAKEAWAYS

1. All families are dysfunctional to a degree.
2. Perspective is healthy, but comparison is not helpful. You have a right to your feelings.
3. The ideal attachment style is secure attachment. Wednesday and Pugsley from *The Addams Family* demonstrate secure attachment.
4. The ideal parenting approach is authoritative parenting. Elastigirl from *The Incredibles* demonstrates authoritative parenting.
5. Instead of thinking of your family as good or bad, think of *emotionally skilled* versus *emotionally unskilled*.
6. You can't make your family change, but you can change how *you* respond to *them*.
7. Boundaries are a necessity for emotionally skillful families.
8. Compassion without boundaries is codependence.
9. Forgiveness is a beautiful spiritual ideal, but it is not required to heal emotional injuries.
10. Unintentionally caused trauma is still trauma. You are *not* crazy.

DOS AND DON'TS

Do	Don't
Remind yourself that all human families are made of people and no people are perfect. Mistakes are inevitable.	Beat yourself up for failing to protect your children from emotional injuries. Skillful parents *attend* to injuries. They do not *avoid* injuries.

Do	Don't
Remember that you can't change your family without their consent.	Try to force your family into the change process. No one in the history of humanity has successfully beat their families into a more skillful way of behaving.
Validate your own feelings and find supportive friends and peers to validate your experiences.	Expect your family to respond to your feelings with empathy.
Take inventory using the language of *skillful* and *unskillful*.	Think you need to blame, shame, or confront your family for their behaviors.

FIVE-MINUTE CHALLENGE

1. Look at the cartoons depicting ten unskillful family dynamics.
2. Make a list of which dynamics feel familiar.
3. For each dynamic on your list, write down the "What to Do . . ." action items.
4. Commit to doing *one* of the suggested action items in the next week.

CHAPTER 8

Trust Your Instruments

How to Recover from Toxic Habits

Don't believe everything you think.

—Robert Fulghum

You know that super-awkward feeling when you're walking down a flight of stairs and miss the last step? Your brain tells you, "Hey, no worries! The ground is level!" but your body says, "NOOOOOOO!" and you trip. After untangling your feet, you furtively glance around to make sure no one saw your gaffe. And if you're unfortunate enough to have witnesses close by, you do a little hop-dance and laugh merrily as if to say, "I *totally* meant to do that."

Now imagine missing that last step is the difference between life and death.

For pilots, a mismatch between what their brain perceives and what's *actually* happening leads to a deadly phenomenon known as the *graveyard spiral*. A graveyard spiral is the result of a physiological process[*] that causes a pilot to *believe* they are flying level. But not only are they *not* flying level, the plane is *rapidly* spiraling toward the ground. Nothing in the pilot's sensory perception feels off. They can neither see nor feel the spiral. This happens not

---

[*] "Spatial disorientation in aircraft can arise from flight situations or visual misinterpretation. . . . If the plane banks or ascends or descends slowly, the pilot may not perceive the change, and the plane will feel level to him." "Spatial Disorientation," *Encyclopaedia Britannica*, https://www.britannica.com/science/spatial-disorientation#ref222226.

because the pilot lacks flying knowledge, but because of an *illusion*. An illusion is a distortion of perception. In other words, what our brains tell us *internally* doesn't match what is happening *externally*. A graveyard spiral is a mismatch between perception and reality. The pilot *thinks* things are fine—but they aren't. The Federal Aviation Administration (FAA) safety brochure says, "If the pilot fails to recognize the illusion and does not level the wings, the airplane will continue . . . losing altitude until it impacts the ground." Other terms for this dangerous spatial disorientation are *deadly spiral* and *vicious spiral*.

Spatial disorientation is something we *all* experience. Your body contains something known as the organ of balance, or what science calls the *vestibular system*. Located in the inner ear, this system is responsible for maintaining balance, posture, and stability. A vestibular *illusion* occurs when there is a disconnect between what is real and what your brain *thinks* is reality. If you've ever sat in the driver's side of a parked car, you've likely experienced a vestibular illusion. Though you're not moving, if the car next to you drives away, you'll reflexively slam on your brakes because it feels like *your* car is rolling forward. The sensory inputs you receive from your brain do *not* reflect the reality around you. Pilots lose control of their aircraft because their perception is not congruent with the situation. According to the FAA handbook, "a pilot's fundamental responsibility is to prevent a loss of control. Loss of control in-flight is the leading cause of fatal general aviation accidents in the U.S. and commercial aviation worldwide."

What does this have to do with your Netflix binges, yo-yo diets, failed New Year's resolutions, or stalled efforts at getting to barre class?

Everything.

Loss of control is the very definition of addiction. While you may not identify as an addict, we all know what it feels like to spin out of control from time to time. As you'll see later in this chapter, addictions are caused by the same thing as graveyard spirals—a mismatch between perception and reality. The key to getting unstuck with addiction or toxic habits can be found in the last place you'd *ever* think to look—aviation safety training. Whether you identify as a hard-core drug user, an emotional eater, or a workaholic, the common denominator is a loss of control that results in a crash. While your compulsions may not be as deadly as chemical addictions or graveyard spirals, the contributing factors are the same.

The FAA handbook also says [italics mine], "To prevent loss-of-control accidents, it is important for pilots to recognize and maintain a heightened awareness of situations that increase the risk of loss-of-control. Disoriented pilots may not always be aware of their orientation error . . . due to some combination of (1) not understanding the *events* as they are unfolding, (2) lacking the *skills* required to alleviate or correct the situation, or (3) exceeding psychological or physiological ability to *cope* with what is happening."

Loss of control with an aircraft or a pack-a-day cigarette habit is the result of an illusion—what we feel *inside* does not match what is happening *outside*. Another word for this in the psychological realm is *denial*. Denial is a refusal to admit to something that we know deep down is true. Rather than confront our pain, we keep our feet firmly planted in the realm of illusion. These illusions manifest in nonchalant claims like "I'll get back on track tomorrow," "I can quit whenever I want to," or "I'm going to start working out this year." New Year's resolutions should really be called New Year's res-*illusions*. You know full well when "one glass" often really means five. I know when I tell myself, *Maybe I'll just eat a* small *bowl of peanut butter Kashi,* I'll end up devouring the box, the bowl, and the spoon. How do we stop lying to ourselves? Let's start by going over the same quote from the FAA handbook with three tiny changes:

> To prevent loss-of-control ~~accidents~~ **behaviors**, it is important for ~~pilots~~ **you** to recognize and maintain a heightened awareness of situations that increase the risk of loss-of-control. Disoriented ~~pilots~~ **people** may not always be aware of their orientation error . . . due to some combination of (1) not understanding the events as they are unfolding, (2) lacking the skills required to alleviate or correct the situation, or (3) exceeding psychological or physiological ability to cope with what is happening.

In order for you to get ~~out of~~ **stuck** with your addictions, compulsions, or habits, we will need to break down the three components outlined in the preceding FAA guidance:

1. Not *understanding* the events as they unfold
2. Lacking *skills* to correct the situation
3. Exceeding *psychological* or *physiological* ability to cope

In the first section (*understanding*), we'll talk about the definition of addiction and the surprising truth about what addiction *isn't*. The second section (*skills*) will give you tools based on fighter pilot strategy. These tools will enable you to get yourself out of stuck and back in control. The third (*psychological/physiological*) covers how to navigate the detox and withdrawal process.

Not Understanding the Events as They Are Unfolding (What Causes Addiction?)

Addiction is like pornography—you know it when you see it. What is the definition? Addiction is a relationship with a substance or behavior that creates an *increase* in tolerance, a *decrease* in control, and continued use despite negative consequences. (You can also substitute the word *habits* for *addiction* if you prefer.) While most people can agree what addiction *looks* like, there is stark disagreement in the research world about what it actually is. The body of academic literature on addiction is wildly inconsistent. You could fill a library with volumes of peer-reviewed research that confidently claims addiction is a medical disease. And you can supply another library with equally valid studies proving addiction is *not* a medical disease. In "What Is a Disease?"* Professor Jackie Leach Skully poses this question: "How do we distinguish properly between real diseases, and human behaviours or characteristics that we just happen to find disturbing?"

---

*Jackie Leach Skully, "What Is a Disease?" *EMBO Reports* 5, no. 7 (2004): 650–53. doi: 10.1038 /sj.embor.7400195.

Addiction is a disease. Addiction isn't a disease. It is. It isn't. It is. Let's consider the following story of one of my former clients.

Pete was one of those kids you hope and pray your daughter or son brings home to marry. As a tall, bright-eyed, sandy-haired seventeen-year-old, he was a varsity football star on the fast track to a promising college career. Pete attended a small Methodist church regularly with his parents and younger sister, volunteered with the local food bank, took annual mission trips with his youth group to build houses, and had *no* history of abuse or mental illness. His *awwwwww* factor could be rivaled only by Zac Efron's character in *High School Musical*. After Pete tore his ACL in a playoff game, his doctor prescribed a powerful and highly addictive opiate painkiller called oxycodone (a.k.a. Oxy). His doctor, like many doctors, did not tell Pete or his family about the addictive properties of opiates. After a few months, Pete was horrified to realize he had become physically dependent on Oxy. When he stopped taking it, severe flu-like symptoms quickly seized his body, including painful muscle cramps, violent vomiting, and profuse sweating. He was too embarrassed to tell his family, so in order to stave off withdrawal symptoms he began to secretly take more and more pills. But Oxy is available only by prescription, and to get it on the street is expensive. Heroin is a cheap alternative. Pete soon found himself living in a house where he and the other occupants shared needles and syringes. Four years later, after he had been arrested multiple times and was sixty pounds lighter, his family intervened and sent him to rehab, where he landed in my office.

Pause for a moment. Do you believe that Pete suffers from a disease?

Yeah, me neither.

Addiction is a complex web of systemic, biological, environmental, and many other factors. There is no simple answer to the question "What is addiction?" Research done on the subject of recovery runs into the same dilemma: just as there's no agreement on the nature of addiction, there is no consistent agreement about which method of recovery works best. Here are just a few reasons people get ensnared by addiction or toxic habits:

▸ Numbing out the present

- Trying to escape the past
- Fear of the future
- Coping with death
- Coping with life
- Dependency as a result of a medically warranted prescription (as was the case with Pete)
- Genetic predisposition
- Mental illness
- Systemic oppression
- Trauma
- Positive reinforcement (the behaviors are continually rewarded, as is often the case with workaholism, obsession with "clean"* food, and exercise addiction)

It's impossible to find a one-size-fits-all solution. We could spend hours examining the neurobiological mechanics of addiction.† We could compare and contrast the models of addiction: the moral model, the disease model, the social learning model, the public health model, and the psychodynamic model.‡ We could debate theories of addiction treatment like abstinence,

---

*The notion of "clean" eating perpetuates toxic diet habits. As authors Elyse Resch and Evelyn Tribole put it in their book *Intuitive Eating*, "The moment you banish a food, it paradoxically builds up a 'craving life' of its own that gets stronger with each diet, and builds more momentum as the deprivation deepens."

† "Three neurobiological circuits have been identified to have heuristic value for the study of neurobiological changes associated with the development and persistence of drug dependence: a binge/intoxication-related circuit, a withdrawal/negative affect–related circuit, and a preoccupation/anticipation (i.e., craving)-related circuit." George F. Koob and Eric P. Zorrilla, "Neurobiological Mechanisms of Addiction: Focus on Corticotropin-Releasing Factor." *Current Opinion in Investigational Drugs* 11, no. 1 (2010): 63. https://www.ncbi.nlm.nih.gov/pmc/articles/PMC2812895/.

‡ The moral model says addiction is a sin. The disease model says the origin of addiction is within a person's brain and cannot be cured. The social learning model says addiction is a learned behavior and can be changed. The public health model says addiction is an interplay among the drug, the user, and the environment. The psychodynamic model says childhood is the origin of addiction. Australian Government, Department of Health, "Models That Help Us Understand AOD Use in Society": https://www1.health.gov.au/internet/publications/publish

harm reduction, and moderation.* While academic theories and research are valuable, you do not need to have a PhD in phenomenology to solve *your* problem of stuck. To break any habit, you need to start with the right question. Pondering the nature of addiction leads down an interesting path of discovery. But it is the *wrong* trailhead if you want to break your unhealthy habits.

What is the right trailhead?

The question you need to ask is not "What is *wrong* with me?" but rather "What is *right* about this behavior?" Most people try to attack habits from the angle of behavior *modification* rather than behavior *comprehension*. Your habits serve a function. Knowing the *function* of your habit is key to changing it. Understanding yourself is the key to breaking bad habits. Remember the pilot example from the beginning of the chapter? Graveyard spirals are *not* caused by a lack of knowledge. Pilots go into the danger zone when they lack *understanding* about what is happening. Noted author Malcolm Gladwell writes in *Blink*, "The key to good decision making is not knowledge. It is understanding. We are swimming in the former. We are desperately lacking in the latter."

> Understanding yourself is the key to breaking bad habits.

Girl Scout cookie binges, margarita benders, marathon viewings of *Grey's Anatomy*—all these behaviors serve a function. Understanding the function opens the door to behavioral change. For a moment, let's suspend the idea that addiction is a disease. (If your fists just clenched, stay with me for a bit longer.) Is addiction *sometimes* a disease? Perhaps. Is it *sometimes* a mental illness? Possibly. Is it *sometimes* a lifelong chronic condition that must be vigorously man-

---

ing.nsf/Content/drugtreat-pubs-front5-wk-toc-drugtreat-pubs-front5-wk-secb-drugtreat-pubs
-front5-wk-secb-3-drugtreat-pubs-front5-wk-secb-3-4#mod.

*Abstinence theory says the only solution is complete avoidance of a substance or behavior. Harm reduction theory tries to mitigate the consequences of addictive behavior using mechanisms like needle exchanges. Moderation theory says that in some cases for some people, a healthy relationship with a chemical or behavior is possible.

aged? Maybe. But more likely than not, if you are reading this book you fall into the camp of people for whom addiction is something else entirely.

What is the something else?

For most of us, addiction is a *protective system of behaviors and illusions we use to guard ourselves from painful truth.** The New England Journal of Medicine says, "The brain disease model is the most prevalent model of addiction in the western world. . . . Learning models propose that addiction, though obviously disadvantageous, is a natural, context-sensitive response to challenging environmental contingencies, not a disease." In *The Biology of Desire: Why Addiction Is Not a Disease*, emeritus professor, cognitive neuroscientist, and developmental psychologist Dr. Marc Lewis writes: "I'm convinced that calling addiction a disease is not only inaccurate, it's often harmful . . . many recovering addicts find it better not to see themselves as helpless victims of a disease, and objective accounts of recovery and relapse suggest they might be right." Dr. Gabor Maté, author of *In the Realm of Hungry Ghosts*, writes: "The discoveries of science, the teachings of the heart, and the revelations of the soul all assure us that no human being is ever beyond redemption. The possibilities of renewal exists so long as life exists. How to support that possibility in others and in ourselves is the ultimate question."

In order to support the possibility of renewal, we need to start with the assumption that even our most toxic habits have the goal of self-protection—*not* self-destruction.† We overeat, under-exercise, overwork, and slack on self-care not because we *hate* ourselves, but because we desperately want to *protect* ourselves. "Protect ourselves from what?" you may wonder. We'll answer that question next.

---

*This chapter is geared toward people for whom this explanation applies. Severe and persistent mental illness, environmental oppression, poverty, and other origins of addiction are *not* the phenomena to which this chapter refers.

†The idea that addiction is a self-protective mechanism does not excuse behaviors. Explanation *never* equals excuse. Explanation is necessary to ignite the change process. No one who struggles with addiction gets to say, "I was protecting myself," as a reason for stealing, lying, and causing chaos in a family.

Lacking Skills to Correct the Situation
(The Truth Shall Set You Free)

The most important skill to break an addiction to snacks, screens, or spending is *not* positive thinking. It is *not* moving your phone into another room (though that can help). It is *not* a strict adherence to the keto diet. And it certainly isn't summoning more willpower. The most important skill to breaking a habit is making an indomitable commitment to your own *truth*.

Ignoring your thoughts is high-risk behavior. How many times a day do you think you lie to yourself? Most people immediately answer that question with earnest protests of "I don't lie!" Let's consider that question again. Lies can be as significant as hiding a porn addiction* or as simple as telling the peppy Trader Joe's crew member you're fine when you're having a day from hell. Withholding your credit card debt from your partner is a lie. So is telling yourself you'll get on the treadmill tomorrow. The gap between *real* and *ideal* is where habits gain power. Like a pilot in a graveyard spiral, when what you think (*I'm fine*) does not match the reality of your situation (*I'm really* not *fine*), eventually you'll crash. Why? Think of what happens when you ignore a minor toothache. You continue to minimize and deny the pain. Eventually your head feels like it's going to explode, and at this point you need a *very* expensive and painful root canal. Ouch. There's a saying in the recovery world that when someone says, "I'm fine," the word *fine* is an acronym for f*cked, insecure, neurotic, and emotional.† Truer words have never been spoken.

> Ignoring your thoughts is high-risk behavior.

---

*The question of whether porn use is healthy is *not* the issue to which this sentence refers. This sentence is about *lying*. The question of whether porn has a place in a sex-positive world is a completely different conversation.

†The origin of this acronym is unknown, but it is often used in Alcoholics Anonymous and

Graveyard spirals are the result of a *spatial* distortion. Addictions are the result of a *truth* distortion. Like a pilot plunging an aircraft to the ground, we unintentionally lead ourselves into catastrophe when we try to sell ourselves on the idea that everything is fine when it is anything *but* fine. Here's a bird's-eye view of the addiction spiral:

THE ADDICTION SPIRAL

- ▸ A bad thing happens.
- ▸ Deny the thing.
- ▸ Avoid the thing.
- ▸ Try to escape the thing using another thing.
- ▸ Feel shame about all the things.
- ▸ Repeat.

How do we break the cycle? Take a look at what happens when we create space for *truth*:

BREAKING THE ADDICTION SPIRAL

- ▸ A bad thing happens.
- ▸ Acknowledge the thing.
- ▸ Feel the pain of the thing.
- ▸ Consider your choices for soothing the pain from the thing.
- ▸ Remind yourself that this is a legitimate thing—you have a right to your pain.
- ▸ Take a deep breath and resist the impulse to do something destructive.

Narcotics Anonymous. The acronym was popularized in the song "F.I.N.E." by Aerosmith on their 1989 album, *Pump*.

Doing an inventory of all your unpleasant/uncomfortable/painful truths is a powerful tool to avert an addiction spiral. Your truth may be as simple as "I'm frustrated with my sister" or as complex as "I want to leave my marriage." Your truth may be coming to terms with your mother's cancer or bravely admitting your seemingly perfect childhood was actually lonely and painful. It may be a secret and long-abandoned desire to paint. Is it possible you don't want to lose weight because you're terrified of sexual attention? Could it be that you fear financial success because you're concerned about appearing materialistic? We hide from truth not because we want to *sabotage* ourselves, but because we want to *defend* ourselves. Use a notebook to copy the chart below. Make a list of anything in your life that has potential to create discomfort. Remember, both good and bad things apply. Avoid the phrase *I should* . . . Do not "should" on yourself.

Areas of Your Life to Examine	Secret Feelings/Thoughts

In *The Body Keeps the Score*, Dr. Bessel van der Kolk writes: "As long as you keep secrets and suppress information, you are fundamentally at war with yourself . . . The critical issue is allowing yourself to know what you know. That takes an enormous amount of courage." We often hide what we know from our conscious awareness because we are terrified that our lives will turn upside down. Here are some fictional examples of what your chart might look like:

Areas of Your Life to Examine	Secret Feelings/Thoughts
Marriage	I'm really unhappy in this marriage. I'm afraid if I admit this, I'll end up alone. But the truth is, I really want a divorce.
Career	I'm worried that my friends will be jealous of my recent promotion. I'm also afraid that my spouse will feel bad that I now outearn them. But the truth is, I really want to celebrate the promotion and enjoy my success.
Creativity	I really want to compose music. I'm afraid if I admit this, I'll end up turning into a starving artist. But the truth is, I'm really angry about never having time to do creative things for myself.
Parenting	Sometimes I feel like running away. I'm afraid if I admit this, that means I'm a terrible parent. But the truth is sometimes I want to tear my hair out and not have to deal with screaming kids.

Your brain whispers seductively, "Forget what you want. Forget what you feel. Forget what you know. It's safer to not know what you know." But the opposite is true. If you want a transformed relationship with food, exercise, alcohol, money, or any other stuck-inducing habit, you'll need to access your truth. You'll also need to look beyond the binary of *abstinent** versus *addicted*.

Breaking habits always requires truth, but it only *sometimes* requires abstinence. For some people in some situations, total abstinence from *all things* for *all time* is a necessity. For some people, abstinence from some things for a *period* of time works best. As we said earlier, there is no one-size-fits-all solution. Consider the following:

Abstinent here means 100 percent avoidance of a substance or behavior.

- You can be abstinent and experience *zero* personal transformation.
- You can experience *massive* personal transformation *without* abstinence.
- Abstinence is *a* pathway to transformation.
- Abstinence is not the *only* pathway to transformation.
- Abstinence does not *equal* transformation.

While there are many beautiful and beneficial gifts of the Twelve-Step program, one of its flaws is an emphasis on character defects rather than a view of addiction as functional and protective. Diet culture would rather you look at your inner *thighs* than at your inner *truth*. And the mindfulness/wellness world often* encourages "good vibes only" at the expense of reality. The absence of truth will always lead to the presence of pathology.

In the 2015 TED talk "Everything You Think You Know About Addiction Is Wrong," speaker/author/journalist Johann Hari made a convincing case for rethinking addiction. In his talk and in his book *Chasing the Scream*, Hari says, "The opposite of addiction isn't sobriety. It's connection." While much of his work is admirable, particularly his compassionate approach to finding solutions and reducing stigma, I disagree with this theory.†

> The absence of truth will always lead to the presence of pathology.

Yes, we are all wired for connection, as we discussed in chapter 6 on friendships. Yes, lack of connection is dangerous to our physical and mental health. However, connection is *not* the silver bullet to eradicate ad-

---

*Note the word *often*. Not *always*. There are plenty of phenomenal wellness and mindfulness people and practices.

†Though I don't subscribe to Hari's theories on addiction, I absolutely *loved* his book *Lost Connections: Why You're Depressed and How to Find Hope*, and highly recommend it.

diction. If connection *was* a magical cure-all, inpatient drug rehab would be largely successful. Why? The rehab world immediately plants people with like-minded companions, meaningful work, daily activities, and 24/7 connection. And yet more often than not, inpatient drug rehab is a revolving door of recovery, relapse, return to treatment, repeat. The CDC website says, "From 1999–2018, over 750,000 people died from a drug overdose. [Drug overdose] was a leading cause of injury-related death in the United States." Clearly our approach to addiction treatment does *not* work.

Connection with other people is a necessary component to recovery. But how often do you feel completely alone in a room full of people? How often do you feel isolated and cut off even while surrounded by friends and family? We often search for meaning in the bodies of other people, in the food we eat, or in things we buy—but it isn't there. The opposite of addiction is *not* connection. The opposite of addiction is *truth*.

What does that mean?

Underneath every addiction, compulsion, bad habit, or problematic behavior is *unaddressed truth*. Martha Beck writes in *Finding Your Own North Star*, "At some point, almost all my clients tell me they don't know what they want, and it's never true. Part of you—your essential self—knows your own desires at every moment of every day (even when the message is a contented 'I want exactly what I have, thank you'). Anytime you think you don't know what you want, it's because your social self has decided you shouldn't want it." Not only does your essential self always know what you want, your essential self always knows when you're in pain—even if you don't think you should be hurting.

Once we unearth the damp moldy basement of the psyche, we almost *always* find painful and unexamined truth. In *The Power of Habit*, Pulitzer Prize–winning journalist Charles Duhigg writes: "It is facile to imply that smoking, alcoholism, overeating, or other ingrained patterns can be upended without real effort. Genuine change requires work and self-understanding of the cravings driving behaviors." Anytime you focus on taming *habits* at the expense of understanding *truth*, you'll likely spin your wheels and stay stuck. Unwanted behaviors almost always leave behind a trail of bread crumbs. The chart below gives you a peek at how triggering events can lead to unhealthy behaviors:

Triggering Event	What We Tell Ourselves	What We Actually Feel	Behavior/Belief
You get into a fight with your mother.	"It's fine. She is who she is."	Ashamed, betrayed, angry, sad	You eat an entire box of cookies and then think your primary issue is food addiction.
Your boss yells at you in front of your peers.	"It's fine. I'm lucky to have a job at all in this economy."	Ashamed, humiliated, angry, sad	You go on a Tinder bender and then think your primary issue is sex addiction.
Your teenager says, "I hate you."	"It's fine. He's just a kid and I don't care what he thinks."	Ashamed, angry, fearful, sad	You spend all your rent money and then think your primary issue is compulsive spending.
The holiday season	"It's fine. It's the most wonderful time of the year."	Resentful, sad, hopeless, lonely	You don't shower for a week and then think your primary issue is laziness.
Someone you love dies.	"It's fine. Everything happens for a reason."	Angry, sad, hopeless, fearful	You drink a bottle of wine and then think your primary issue is alcoholism.

When clients come to sessions bewildered by or ashamed of their choices, the first order of business is to break the illusion that their behavior is the primary issue. How? Using the same examples from the chart above, let's examine what might be *really* going on below the surface.

Behavior/Belief	What Is the Truth?
You eat an entire box of cookies and then think your primary issue is food addiction.	You hate fighting with your mother. Sometimes you wonder if she ever really wanted to have you. But you feel bad even thinking this. Overeating provides you comfort. Focusing solely on food addiction is an effective distraction from dealing with pain.
You go on a Tinder bender and then think your primary issue is sex addiction.	When your boss yelled at you, the public humiliation made you remember when you were routinely verbally abused as a child. You try not to think about that, so instead you end up acting out with other people so you can feel more in control. Focusing solely on sex addiction is a way to avoid underlying trauma.
You spend all your rent money and then think your primary issue is compulsive spending.	When your teenager yells at you, you feel like a terrible parent. Sometimes you try to make up for it by buying things even if you don't need them. Then you focus solely on your financial problems so you don't have to feel shame and inadequacy about your parenting challenges.
You don't shower for a week and then think your primary issue is laziness.	The holiday season can be depressing and difficult. It's hard for you to find people who understand why you don't want to celebrate. So you feel hopeless and end up doing nothing. Then you obsess about how lazy you are instead of thinking about how lonely and isolated you feel.
You drink a bottle of wine and then think your primary issue is alcoholism.	Someone you loved very much just died in a car crash. You're grieving and have no one to talk to about this. A sole focus on your drinking habits provides a way to avoid the grieving process.

Addictions and compulsive habits are problematic and need to be managed, but the primary issue is unaddressed truth. When you know what you're *really* thinking and feeling, you can apply interventions that deactivate impulsivity and improve your sense of "I can do this." Knowing the source of your pain is required to heal that pain and control your habits. In *The War of Art*, author Steven Pressfield writes: "Our job in this life is not to shape ourselves into some ideal we imagine we ought to be, but to find out who we already are and become it." What are some of the ways you try to shape-shift out of your own truth and into an idealized image? You'll probably recognize some of these thought distortions:

- It wasn't *that* bad.
- They didn't mean to hurt me.
- This is a silly thing to be upset about.
- I should just be grateful.

It is healthy to recognize privilege, to feel gratitude for resources, and to have perspective about the good things in your life. But remember, perspective is healthy, comparison is *not*. Comparison distorts truth. Just like a body of water needs an inlet and an outlet or else it gets stagnant and contaminated, so too do we need to balance perspective with pain. When perspective comes at the expense of truth, it quickly turns infectious. You can't prevent a root canal if you don't admit to your toothache. The first task to breaking a habit or addiction is admitting to your truth—you are not fine. The second task is to pose the question: "Okay, so I admit I'm not fine. I admit I'm in pain. Now what?" The answer to this question can be found in a surprising place—a military concept known as the OODA loop.

The OODA Loop

In the 1950s, Colonel John Boyd, a U.S. Air Force fighter pilot, a Pentagon consultant, and a military strategist, created the OODA loop—Observe, Orient, Decide, Act.* Whatever habit you hope to break, this simple four-part tool can help you get *out* of stuck and stay *in* control. In *Boyd: The Fighter Pilot Who Changed the Art of War*, author Robert Coram writes: "Boyd . . . realized . . . every person experiences some form of war. . . . To prevail in personal and business relations, and especially war, we must understand what takes place in a person's mind." If you bristle at the "life is sometimes a war" idea, take a peek at your language. As we saw in chapter 1, war metaphors abound. We *battle* the scale, *fight* destructive impulses, and experience *nuclear meltdowns*. You may sometimes think you're your own worst *enemy*. Your home may feel like a *combat zone*. As you learned in chapter 2, changing or challenging your thoughts (as with cognitive behavioral therapy) can change the trajectory of your behavior. The OODA loop framework is a mindfulness technique. When you bring mindful awareness to your thoughts, you escape the trap of automatic thinking and behaving.

▸ Observe

Pause. Notice your impulse to procrastinate/drink/binge/etc. Consider the events of today and the previous week. Ask yourself if you are lying to yourself about anything. Then ask yourself again: *What do I really think and feel about the events of the recent past? Are there any situations I need to examine for secret thoughts and feelings and unaddressed pain?*

---

*The OODA loop is a highly complex military strategy *heavily* modified here for the purpose of breaking habits. Variations of the OODA loop are often used in the litigation and business worlds to improve decision-making skills.

▸ Orient

Notice you live inside a body. Where in your body are you feeling discomfort? What are you feeling compelled to do? Notice the sensations of hot, cold, numb, buzzy, tingling, or tension. Notice your heart rate, breathing, and temperature. Remind yourself that your body is trying to help you and is *not* trying to sabotage you.

▸ Decide

Ask yourself, *What are my choices right now?* Make a list of all the people, places, and things available to you. How can you use your resources to help you feel slightly less triggered? What actions might you take? Organize the list from the easiest to the most difficult to execute.

▸ Act

Do the first thing on the list. If that action doesn't help you resist your impulse, do the second action. Continue until you reach the end of your list. If you are still feeling impulsive, return to the Observe step and repeat the process.

YOUR OODA LOOP: COPY INTO A NOTEBOOK

Observe: What do I really think about this situation?

Orient: What is going on inside my body?

Decide: What are my choices?

Act: How did making that decision feel? Do I need to do anything else?

The OODA loop prevents emotional spirals. You may be quick to ignore or minimize little irritants and "minor" daily annoyances, but unaddressed pain *rapidly* picks up speed and velocity. Sooner or later you'll find yourself spinning out of control. As you work your own OODA loop, it can be helpful to remember the words of English literature icon Samuel Johnson: "The chains of habit are too weak to be felt until they are too strong to be broken."

Exceeding Psychological or Physiological Ability to Cope

The first part of our discussion from the FAA manual focused on understanding addiction's function—self-protection. The second part provided skills to correct and avoid a dangerous situation using truth and the OODA loop. The third and final part covers what to do when psychological and physiological factors exceed your ability to cope. You get addicted to substances and habits because as soon as you try to stop, your body is overwhelmed with impulsive urges. Your brain tries to cope, but eventually you give in to cravings. Withdrawal is the unpleasant but necessary step between *Yay, I made a good decision!* and *Yay, I have a healthy new habit!* Withdrawal isn't just for users of hard drugs. It can happen with *anything* your brain is used to having—people, places, things, behaviors, or substances. Withdrawal symptoms can range from mild discomfort to debilitating panic and physiological symptoms like nausea or migraines.[*] You are *not* crazy. In order to change a habit, you need to prepare to deal with the withdrawal and detox stage. One of the biggest stuck-ifying myths is the belief that making good *decisions* immediately produces good *feelings*. This is an illusory expectation. As you'll recall from the section on graveyard spirals, illusions quickly lead to crashes. Here are the ten stages you can count on when you set out to break a long-standing habit. Buckle your seat belt.

THE STAGES OF BREAKING A HABIT

1. Ready. Let's do this.
2. Yay. I'm making a healthy change.
3. Ouch.
4. No, seriously . . . ouch.

---

[*] Always check with a medical doctor first to rule out medical reasons for your symptoms.

5. I want to give up.

6. Sigh . . . fine.

7. This is boring.

8. I'm depressed.

9. I think I'm feeling less bad.

10. This doesn't suck.

In *The Princess Bride*, one of the most quoted lines is from the hero Westley, who snarkily observes, "Life *is* pain, Highness. Anyone who says differently is selling something." You could slightly modify that to say, "*Habit-breaking* is pain. Anyone who says differently is selling something." Don't let the "good vibes always" claims trick you into thinking you're alone in your struggle. Quitting a toxic person, chemical, or behavior is *really* hard in the initial days and weeks. If our expectations are too lofty ("This is going to be great!") we will bail when painful reality hits. When expectations ("This is going to suck") match reality ("Yep, this really sucks"), you can stay in control using your OODA loop. It's helpful to also keep in mind that *meh* is a point on the path to feeling good. As you adjust to your new habits, you'll likely enter a period of feeling numb. This is a normal part of the process. Though it's tempting at this point to mistake feeling numb for feeling *depressed*, stay the course.

"Okay, I'll stay the course . . . but how long is this going to take?"

Pop psychology often claims it takes twenty-one days* to build a shiny new habit. Because there are so many factors that go into the change process (age, health, access to resources, financial stability, motivation, genetics, etc.), it is nearly impossible to give a habit-breaking timeline. A study published in the *European Journal of Social Psychology* found that some participants changed habits in as little as eighteen days, others as long as 254 days.

---

*The figure of twenty-one days is often cited in pop culture and has its likely origin in a 1960s book on self-image called *Psycho-Cybernetics* by plastic surgeon Dr. Maxwell Maltz. Dr. Maltz did not say it takes twenty-one days to form a habit. He said it usually took at least three weeks for his patients to form a new self-image.

Regardless of how long it really takes to change a habit, you can be assured that withdrawal does *not* last forever. Based on anecdotal reports, assuming you exist in a relatively functional environment, most people experience noticeable relief from habit withdrawal by the end of the second week. If you are currently addicted to a chemical, seek medical attention. It can be dangerous and even life-threatening to detox off certain drugs and alcohol without medical supervision. The anecdotal reports here refer to changing patterns of *behavior*—not to tapering off substances. If you are considering inpatient treatment for yourself or a loved one, it is important to research and spend time finding a qualified facility and making sure to create a plan for aftercare.

Conclusion

My own recovery story includes drug abuse, eating disorders, obsessive-compulsive spirals, and dangerous behavioral addictions. It's not *easy* to break habits, but the process is *simple*. Whatever issue *you* face, the skill set required to change a habit is the same skill set used to prevent a plane crash—understanding what is *real* versus believing what we *feel*. This takes a little bit of training and practice but is well worth the effort. You'd think that new pilots would be required to learn how to avoid graveyard spirals. They aren't. You'd also think schools would train kids how to identify and challenge thought distortions. They don't. But you *can* retrain your brain. How? The FAA handbook says, "If you experience a vestibular illusion during flight, trust your instruments and disregard your sensory perceptions." On an aircraft, the *attitude indicator* is an instrument that gives pilots a clear picture of their position relative to the horizon. Your OODA loop chart is your attitude indicator. Rather than blindly trusting what you think, take the time to make sure your perceptions match your reality.

Recovering from addictions and bad habits isn't about being good or denying yourself pleasure. Recovery is about *honesty*. As author Robert Fulghum wisely noted, "Don't believe everything you think." As long as you stay honest about your thoughts and feelings and avoid illusions, you likely *won't* get stuck on the couch or inside a can of Pringles. Recovery is owning your life and challenging *illusions*.

In *Awakening the Heroes Within*, author Carol S. Pearson writes: "No life, no matter how successful and exciting it might be, will make you happy if it is not really your life. And no life will make you miserable if it is genuinely your own." Remind yourself that seeing *isn't* always believing. In Madeleine L'Engle's beloved classic, *A Wrinkle in Time*, the protagonist Meg tries in vain to describe vision to the sightless creature known as Aunt Beast. Aunt Beast, bewildered by the concept, keenly replies, "We don't know what things *look* like. We know what things *are* like. It must be a very limiting thing, this seeing."

How right she was.

Bottom-Line Takeaways

1. Lying to yourself is the fuel that keeps addictions and habits alive.
2. There is not a one-size-fits-all cure for addiction.
3. Addictions and habits are problematic, but they are not *the* problem.
4. The goal of your addictions and habits is self-protection, *not* self-sabotage.
5. The opposite of addiction is *honesty*.
6. Abstinence is *not* the only way to manage addictions and habits.
7. Underneath every addiction, compulsion, and habit is unaddressed pain.
8. Making a good *decision* rarely produces an immediate good *feeling*.
9. *Withdrawal* is the step between wanting and having.
10. *Do not attempt to withdraw from chemicals without medical supervision.*

DOS AND DON'TS

Do	Don't
Make an end-of-the-day list (in your head is fine) and ask, *Where was I dishonest with myself or someone else?*	Think that you didn't lie today. We all lie every day. Teeny-tiny lies count as lies.
Answer this question honestly: "I don't always do the things I know I could do to feel better because _____."	Beat yourself up for not doing the things you know to do. If it was easy to break habits, there wouldn't be any habits to break.
Ask yourself where you have unaddressed pain (even if you don't think you should be in pain about it).	Worry about making changes all at once. One step at a time.
Prepare yourself for the withdrawal process by creating an inventory of people, places, and things that will help you endure the weeks of discomfort.	Give up when withdrawal hits. It's tough to make it through the discomfort, but acute withdrawal from bad habits (excluding chemicals) rarely lasts more than a week or two.

FIVE-MINUTE CHALLENGES

1. Gratitude is healthy only if it coexists with truth. Make a list of ten things for which you are grateful.

2. On the other side of your gratitude list, make another list of ten things with which you are frustrated, annoyed, angry, or sad. (Even if you feel like you shouldn't be frustrated, annoyed, angry, or sad.)

3. At the end of the day, think of at least *one* lie you told to yourself or someone else. Don't judge yourself, just notice.

CHAPTER 9

Becoming an Emotional Adult

Little Alice fell
d
o
w
n
the hOle,
bumped her head
and bruised her soul

—Lewis Carroll, *Alice's Adventures in Wonderland*

Olivia walked into my office looking camera-ready as usual. The black pencil skirt and crisp white shirt created a striking canvas for the tasteful jewelry draped elegantly around her neck and wrists. Her flawless makeup was framed by glossy hair in salon-perfect waves. But contrary to her *Vogue*-worthy appearance, Olivia was a terrified little girl inside the body of a grown woman.

After grabbing my weighted blanket and a box of Kleenex, Olivia settled onto the couch in my office and tearfully described her latest dating crisis. Though she was thirty-nine, she was as baffled by life as little Alice blundering through Wonderland. Olivia never said what she meant and rarely meant what she said. She said no when she wanted to say yes and yes when she wanted to say no. Boundaries? Impossible. Her father ruled her life (and her finances) with the same ferocity that the Queen of Hearts demanded heads. Olivia lived in constant terror that her friends would abandon her. And though she was a well-respected tax attorney, she never followed through on the things she *knew* would make her feel better. Olivia, like Alice, "generally gave herself very good advice (though she very seldom followed it)."

The clinical term for Olivia's perpetual adolescence is *emotional regression*.* Emotional regression is the thing that happens when you feel physically smaller and emotionally younger than your chronological age. Your emotional "size" doesn't match your actual size. This chapter is all about emotional regression—what it is, why you get stuck, and the path to transform from emotional regression into emotional adulthood. As an emotional adult you won't need to play small anymore. You won't take orders from the mean voices in your head (referred to by some as the "itty-bitty shitty committee").† And a bonus—as an emotional adult you'll have power to turn your all-powerful parents back into regular human *people*. When you know what regression is and how to reverse it, you can get out of stuck and into motion.

Naming the Problem—Emotional Regression Versus Emotional Adulthood

Do you ever feel scared that you'll get "in trouble" at work? Are you afraid to upset your parents? Until I was *twenty-seven* I hid my tattoos under leotards so as not to incur my father's wrath. Do adult tasks like oil changes or teeth cleanings cause overwhelm and paralysis?

Do you feel the need to ask permission from your partner like you would

---

* "Regression in adults . . . entails retreating to an earlier developmental stage (emotionally, socially, or behaviorally)" in times of stress. Hermioni N. Lokko and Theodore A. Stern. "Regression: Diagnosis, Evaluation, and Management." *The Primary Care Companion for CNS Disorders* 17, no. 3 (2015): 10.4088/PCC.14f01761. https://doi.org/10.4088/PCC.14f01761.

† The origin of the term *itty-bitty shitty committee* is unknown, but it's an expression commonly used in recovery circles. The itty-bitty shitty committee is the group of critical voices in your head from whom you fear judgment.

a parent? The chart below shows the difference between emotional regression and emotional adulthood.

Signs of Emotional Regression	Signs of Emotional Adulthood
Indecisiveness.	Emotional adults solicit feedback and weigh options, but ultimately feel empowered to make decisions.
Fear of making people angry.	Emotional adults do not take on the responsibility of managing other people's feelings. Emotional adults navigate conflict skillfully and can set boundaries.
Can't say no.	Confidently says no.
Emotional explosions.	Emotional regulation. Responsive rather than reactive.
Wants to be the "favorite" child, employee, or friend.	Knows that all people have value and that life isn't a zero-sum game.
Never feels competent. Impostor syndrome.	Owns their weaknesses and strengths.
Fear of following dreams—what will "other people" think?	Confidently moves in the direction of their dreams even if it means disappointing people.

In order to get out of stuck, you need to stay right-sized. The struggle to stay right-sized is *real*. Lewis Carroll seemed to understand emotional regression when he wrote *Alice's Adventures in Wonderland*. Alice tells the Caterpillar, "being so many different sizes in a day is very confusing." How many times a day do you experience different sizes? Think about it. You might shrink in fear when your boss calls you into her office but later that evening feel like a capable grown-up as you read to your sleepy child. You may feel like a moody sixteen-year-old the morning your mother criticizes your weight, but by midafternoon you are a powerful warrior who *killed it* at the sales meeting. We all experience size-shifting to varying degrees. When emotional regression is activated, adults morph into crying infants, sullen teenagers, or screaming toddlers.

It's The Most Wonderful Time of the Year . . . for Regression

Consider the emotional climate from Thanksgiving to New Year's Eve. As we discussed in chapter 7 on family dynamics, no time of year provides more evidence of emotional regression than the holiday season.* The holiday season is for therapists what tax season is for accountants. Phones light up, email in-boxes fill to overflowing, and waiting lists balloon. How young do you feel when you go home for the holidays? The chasm between cultural expectations and the reality of the holiday season is wide and deep. Emotional pain gets stuffed down (along with lots of pumpkin pie and eggnog) because people think they should be happy. Think of the 24/7 stream of cheery messages:

- ▸ "'Tis the season to be jolly . . ."
- ▸ "Joy to the world . . ."
- ▸ "Rejoice! Rejoice!"
- ▸ "All is calm, all is bright . . ."
- ▸ "Peace on earth, goodwill to men . . ."

Despite the positive and encouraging soundtrack in the background, the holiday season is when depression skyrockets and self-esteem plummets. Emotional regression isn't the *only* cause of the holiday blues, but it falls *high* on the list of contributing factors. How often do you begrudgingly attend your sister's holiday party when what you *really* want is a solo evening? If you tell your sister yes because you're fearful of her temper, that's a sign of emotional regression. How many times have you dragged yourself through an-

---

*This chapter references several specific U.S. holidays but applies to any holiday for any religion in any region.

other Thanksgiving fiasco with your partner's family when what you'd *rather* do is stay home and order takeout? If you say yes only to appease your icy mother-in-law, emotional regression is likely the cause. Most of us spend November and December feeling small and stuck. Then on New Year's Day we return to our correct size and make determined resolutions. When spring rolls around and we've long abandoned those resolutions, we feel shame. When the holidays roll around again, the cycle starts anew. Regress. Resolve. Repeat.

In *Growing Yourself Back Up*, expert John Lee writes: "Regression is so widespread in our culture that most people are either in the process of regressing, are in the middle of a regression, or have recently come out of a regression. . . . Learning to deal with regression in yourself and others is one of the most valuable skills you will ever learn." If you're feeling stuck in *any* area of your life, it is likely that emotional regression plays a starring role. To begin the process of "growing yourself back up," think of all the people, places, and events that cause you to feel younger than your chronological age. You can use this format (or create your own) to compile an inventory. Copy the following phrases into a notebook (repeat as many times as needed) to create your "regression list":

I feel _____ years old when my _____ (*mother/father/ boss/spouse/friend*) says/does_____. If I felt grown and powerful, I would say/do _____ instead. But I don't because I'm afraid _____ will happen.

We'll return to your list later in the chapter. The next section highlights what *should* happen—successful transformation from emotional childhood to emotional adulthood. (Try not to shame yourself if your transformation feels incomplete—you're in good company.) Then we'll dive into the cause of emotional regression and challenge the beliefs that contribute to staying stuck. Finally, you'll get access to the trail map that leads out of emotional regression. Warning—this path takes a bit of work, but the endgame rewards make the work worth doing.

Adulthood Interrupted—
The Alchemy of Adolescence

Alchemy is a mythical process of transformation. According to the Royal Society of Chemistry, "The aims of the alchemists were threefold: to find the Stone of Knowledge (The Philosopher's Stone), to discover the medium of Eternal Youth and Health, and to discover the transmutation of metals [turning lead into gold]." In many spiritual traditions, alchemy is used as a metaphor to describe the process of turning pain into power, messes into messages, and trauma into triumph. From raw materials the alchemist attempts to create something of infinite value. Alchemy is a magical and mysterious process.

So is growing up.

In the acclaimed novel *The Alchemist*, author Paulo Coelho's protagonist says, "This is why alchemy exists . . . so that everyone will search for his treasure, find it, and then want to be better than he was in his former life." Alchemy is a way to describe your developmental journey from childhood to adulthood. You didn't get to choose your childhood, but you *do* get to decide what to do with the raw material. Adolescence is (ideally) the time when the raw material of childhood is processed and transformed into a gloriously functional adulthood. But this process is almost *always* interrupted. Life happens. This is *not* your fault. Alchemical interruption is not a personal weakness. Caregivers, finances, privilege, trauma, and myriad factors outside your control contribute to the process.

Because there are no clear lines differentiating childhood from adulthood, it's impossible to magically transform into an adult in *every* area of your life simultaneously. You may be an amazing parent, yet a tenth-grader could rival your financial fluency. You may perform your job brilliantly but struggle to make yourself floss.* You may have no trouble maintaining

---

* If you have secret "hygiene shame," know that a staggering number of otherwise high-functioning adults report issues with brushing, flossing, or showering.

friendships but find intimacy terrifying. Most of us get stuck in *at least* one area of our lives.

In *Alchemy: How Adolescence Changes Children into Adults*, Dr. Harris C. Faigel writes: "Adolescence, like alchemy, is an almost magical process that transforms children into adults. It is a personal passage through time, a difficult and demanding journey of exploration, at times stormy, at times dull. Adolescence is the bridge, the alchemic change that makes the journey from childhood to adulthood happen." If adolescence is the bridge to adulthood, the bridge is crammed with travelers stuck in transit. Regression into "adolescent brain" is the culprit behind many explosions, meltdowns, and freak-outs.

Fortunately, since emotional regression is a state of mind and not a physical condition, you *don't* have to stay on the bridge. As Einstein said, "Time and space are modes by which we think and not conditions in which we exist." If time and space are thoughts, that means you have the power to change them.* It is absolutely possible to reverse emotional regression and return to emotional adulthood. Alice fell down the rabbit hole, then emotionally grew up and found her way home. You can do the same.

What Causes Regression?

Emotional regression is caused by psychological homesickness. What does that mean? Maya Angelou wrote: "The ache for home lives in all of us. The safe place where we can go as we are and not be questioned." But home is not just the brick-and-mortar structure where cheeky decor instructs you to "live, laugh, love."† Richelle E. Goodrich wrote: "Home is where '*I know you*,'

---

* Disclaimer: "Change your thoughts, change your life" is true *only* if you are safe, are *not* subject to systemic racism, and have access to resources. This is not true for everyone. If there are areas where you legitimately have zero power to change, focus on changing what you can.

† A Google search for "live, laugh, love" returns 457 *million* results and thousands upon thousands of wall hangings, tchotchkes, and coffee mugs.

'*I accept you*,' '*I forgive you*,' and '*I love you*' are most likely to be heard." The most important person you need to hear these sentiments from is *you*. Adults who feel psychologically "homesick" emotionally regress and search *outside* for what can be found only *inside*. Until it feels safe to live in your mind and body, no place will ever truly feel like home.

You may physically live at home with your parents or extended family. You may physically create a home with your partner and children. There's nothing wrong with that. But to get out of stuck, home needs to *also* be an inside job. Feminist trailblazer Betty Friedan said, "It is easier to live through someone else than to complete yourself. The freedom to lead and plan your own life is frightening if you have never faced it before. It is frightening when a woman finally realizes that there is no answer to the question 'who am I' except the voice inside herself." The journey to know yourself as a fully grown adult—of any gender—is a hero's journey.

The hero's journey is a concept popularized by Joseph Campbell. Most of our favorite stories use this motif. The hero leaves home, encounters obstacles, then triumphantly returns home wiser and more mature, and with a deeper understanding of herself. In *The Hero with a Thousand Faces*, Campbell wrote: "The journey of the hero is about the courage to seek the depths; the image of creative rebirth; the eternal cycle of change within us; the uncanny discovery that the seeker is the mystery which the seeker seeks to know." The point of the hero's journey is to transform from emotional childhood into emotional adulthood. You'll know you're nearing your destination when:

- ▸ Your tolerance for toxic relationships decreases.
- ▸ Your relationships with food, sleep, and sex feel (mostly) peaceful.
- ▸ You say what you mean (and mean what you say) without fear of judgment.
- ▸ You own your no.
- ▸ Your self-talk is compassionate and kind.

- You feel empowered to make decisions.
- You no longer fear "getting in trouble."
- You take your own advice.

At this point clients usually say, "Okay, this is sort of making sense. I'm stuck because I don't feel like an adult. I don't feel at home in my body. Got it. But now what? How do I find my way home?"

Beliefs That Block the Transition to Emotional Adulthood

The first thing to do after naming the problem (emotional regression) is to identify the beliefs that keep you stuck on the bridge to adulthood. In chapters 5 and 6, you learned to differentiate between child and adult relationships. We'll use that same differentiation process here. There are four primary beliefs that block the transition from emotional childhood to emotional adulthood:*

1. **Unconditional Love** (the belief that adults get to give and receive it)
2. **Unconditional Trust** (the belief that adult relationships need it)
3. **Goodness** (the belief in good guys and bad guys)
4. **Innocence** (the belief that life is nothing but unicorns and butterflies)

---

*Not every child gets to experience these beliefs. I didn't, and you may not have either. Childhood trauma destroys the ability to believe in innocence, goodness, and unconditional love and trust. If your circumstances deprived you of the gifts of childlike thinking, skip to the next section.

Childhood Ideal	Adult Reality
I get unconditional love!	In *The Drama of the Gifted Child,* psychologist and bestselling author Alice Miller wrote: "As adults we don't need unconditional love . . . this is a childhood need, one that can never be fulfilled later in life." *All* healthy expressions of love require conditions. The only person who can give you unconditional love as an adult is *you*.
I have unconditional trust in people!	All people are human, and no humans are perfect. Chapter 6 dismantles the myth that unconditional trust is necessary—or realistic—for healthy adult relationships.
Goodness is a thing! Life has good guys and bad guys.	There are no all-good or all-bad people. Emotional adults recognize that inside *all* of us is a balance of good and not-so-good.
Innocence is a thing! Nothing bad or unfair happens in life!	Innocence is a gift available to only a small group of *very* fortunate children. Emotional adults can experience childlike wonder and joy, but not innocence. Innocence as an adult is incompatible with acknowledging the reality of pain. Emotional adults are aware of the harsher realities of life.

Before you throw this book across the room in protest, remember that the rewards of adulthood *far* outweigh the perks of childhood. It's painful to outgrow childhood ideals, but as an emotional adult you get to decide:

- Who to date or befriend
- What to eat, how much, and when
- Where to live (and where to spend holidays)
- How to parent your own kids
  (human *and* fur babies)
- When to follow your dreams

And remember—you don't have to leave *everything* behind in childhood. Quite the contrary. As an emotional adult you'll have *more* freedom to dream and indulge in whimsical desires. (I myself built a secret bookshelf door that opens to a hidden reading nook—a childhood fantasy inspired by Nancy Drew.) The legendary Julia Cameron, known as the Queen of Change and creatrix of *The Artist's Way*, devised a method called "artist dates" that can help if you feel creatively stuck. "The artist date is a once weekly, festive, solo expedition to explore something that interests you."* Emotional adults give themselves guilt-free permission to do things like artist dates. Emotional adulthood does *not* require you to abandon childlike wonder, imagination, or magic. But emotional adulthood *does* require you to recognize that the *developmental stage* of childhood is over.

You can still gleefully tear open brightly colored holiday presents as an adult. You can play with LEGOs to your heart's content and eat Cheerios in front of Saturday-morning cartoons. You can paint your ceiling purple and your walls blue. You can splash in puddles, build epic blanket forts, play dress-up, and chase fireflies. We all have an "inner child" who loves to explore and play.

And.

Chronologically, you will never again be a ten-year-old hoping for Dad to come home and play catch.† You'll never get to relive the excitement of a five-year-old wishing on birthday candles or a tween nervously preparing for a first kiss. If your childhood was painful, you don't get to go back and redo it. If your childhood was joyful, you don't get to stay there. Emotional regression is the result of either:

---

* "Artist Dates." *https://juliacameronlive.com/basic-tools/artists-dates/*. If not for *The Artist's Way*, I'd likely still be at a job I loathed, in a relationship that was destroying me, and addicted to all manner of chemicals and behaviors. Julia Cameron's tools and concepts are life-changing. Highly recommend.

† If you believe in reincarnation, then technically yes, you do get another shot at childhood. But that'll be a different childhood. Reincarnation is *not* a "get out of jail free" card from pain in *this* life.

(A) Trying to remain a child (if your childhood was happy)

or

(B) Trying to re-create childhood (if your childhood was less than ideal)

Olivia, the client described at the beginning of this chapter, was stuck because she desperately longed to continue to be "Daddy's little girl." Emotional regression gave Olivia the *illusion* of unconditional love and care—but at a very high price. Her alchemical transformation was interrupted by the belief that she needed to be "rescued." In the Becoming an Emotional Adult workshops I teach with mindset maven Dr. Sasha Heinz (who wrote the foreword to this book and is one of my favorite people on the planet), we guide courageous travelers through the winding and often uncomfortable road out of emotional regression. As an emotional adult, you do *not* need a "white knight"—you *are* the white knight.*

What does that mean? One tool to reverse emotional regression—and a road that can lead you home—is *grief*.

Record scratch.

Wait, what? The solution to regression is grief?

Grief is a dirty word in the "just think positive" wellness world. You're not supposed to grieve unless someone is dead, and even then you're allowed only a brief window of time before you're expected to "move on and live your life." Grief is the secret weapon that breaks the spell of regression. Grief frees you from the chains of the past. Grief opens the door that leads to your most authentic, adult, magical self.

How?

Grieving the past frees you from the compulsion to repeat it.† If your

---

*Being your own white knight does not mean you don't still need other people. We are all wired for connection. There is a difference between reaching out for *help* and reaching out for *rescue*.

†*Repetition compulsion* is a Freudian concept popularized and updated in the work of trauma expert Dr. Bessel van der Kolk.

childhood was traumatic, grief work helps you to metabolize the trauma. If your childhood was decent or happy, grief work is still necessary. Why? Grief work allows your brain to process the expiration of unconditional love, trust, goodness, and innocence. Grief work tells your brain, "The

> Grieving the past frees you from the compulsion to repeat it.

time to be fully cared for by someone *else* is over—it is *your* turn to take the reins." The transformation from your emotional childhood to emotional adulthood requires you to honor the past and lay it to rest. *All* significant endings require a grieving process.

Grief Work—The Path That Leads You Home

Father of attachment theory and psychiatrist John Bowlby wrote: "Adults who show prolonged absence of conscious grieving are commonly self-sufficient people, proud of their independence and self-control. . . . But sooner or later some of those who avoid all conscious grieving break down—usually with some form of depression." If you are stuck in any area of your life, a degree of conscious grieving is a necessary and powerful tool.

But modern Western culture is really bad at grief.

Grief is uncomfortable because it reminds us of our vulnerability. Grief doesn't care about power, status, or wealth. Grief—at some point—pays a visit to us all.

In *It's OK That You're Not OK*, author Megan Devine writes: "What we need to remember—as a working practice—is to honor all griefs. Honor all losses, small and not small. Life changing and moment changing. And then, not to compare them. That all people experience pain is not medicine for anything." The end of your childhood—whether good or bad—falls into the category of griefs to honor. Even if you can't remember anything about your

> The past stays present until it's processed.

childhood, it is important to tell yourself, *This period of my life is over. I don't get to go back and redo it. I no longer belong in childhood. I give myself permission to feel all my feelings and to grieve all losses great and small.*

Emotional regression happens when we refuse to accept the finality of childhood. But even if you *do* accept childhood's passing, misinformation about grief can render you stuck. If mental health is a commitment to reality (as you read in chapter 1), it's important to separate myth from reality when it comes to the grieving process.

GRIEF MYTH VS. GRIEF REALITY

"Time heals all wounds."	Time does not heal all wounds. You can experience intense feelings about something that happened two, five, or twenty years ago. *The healing process* is what heals wounds—not the passage of time.
"You need to have closure."	Closure is *not* dependent on another person. Closure is an *internal* process. It's about your relationship to *yourself*. Closure does not depend on someone else to be willing, apologetic, or alive.
"Don't speak ill of the dead."	This advice is from the sixth century BC philosopher Chilon of Sparta.* Times have changed. You're allowed to be mad at dead people. * Fun fact: Chilon's advice was later popularized as a Latin proverb: *De mortuis nihil nisi bonum.* https://www.washingtonpost.com/science/2018/08/28/when-ancient-taboo-speaking-ill-dead-goes-online/.
"You need to leave the past in the past."	The past stays present until it's processed. The past is in your body. You carry every experience you've ever had.
"You need to forgive to heal."	Forgiveness is a spiritual ideal, but it is not required to heal trauma or to process grief.

GRIEF MYTH VS. GRIEF REALITY

"You need to let it go."	Episodic memories (things we remember) are stored in our bodies. You can't "let them go." Your experiences become part of your physiology.
"You can't change the past."	You can't change anything about the past—but you can change everything about how your brain stores your memories from the past.
"They never meant to hurt me, so I shouldn't feel bad."	Intention doesn't cancel impact. I may not have meant to hit you with my car, but that doesn't unbreak your leg.
"Grief happens in five stages."	Elisabeth Kübler-Ross's theory of the "five stages of grief" is about dying—not grieving. Her work focused on terminal patients preparing for death, *not* on loved ones dealing with loss. Grief is a messy swirl—up and down, back and forth—with no rhyme or reason to it. There are no neat and clean stages.

The last point on the above chart is worth repeating: grief does *not* happen in stages, and yet most people are still taught the "five stages of grief" model. The model of the five stages is about dying, not grieving. Instead of stages, consider the "task" approach designed by J. William Worden.* Worden's Four Tasks of Grieving model is the current gold standard for therapists, coaches, and counselors. We'll modify Worden's language to fit the challenge of grieving childhood, but here are the tasks in their original form:

WORDEN'S FOUR TASKS OF GRIEVING

   1. To accept the reality of the loss
   2. To process the pain of grief

---

* The Four Tasks of Grieving are from *Grief Counseling and Grief Therapy: A Handbook for the Mental Health Practitioner* by J. William Worden.

3. To adjust to a world without the deceased
4. To find an enduring connection with the deceased while embarking on a new life

As Alice Miller puts it: "Experience has taught us that we have only one enduring weapon in our struggle against mental illness: the emotional discovery and emotional acceptance of the truth in the individual and unique history of our childhood."

> The goal of grieving is to find your way home to yourself.

You may not struggle with a mental illness, but we *all* know the discomfort of feeling stuck. The "enduring weapon" in your struggle against stuckness is the willingness to accept the truth that childhood—no matter how great or awful—is over. Only then can you cross the bridge leading from childhood to adulthood. The goal of grieving isn't to change the past. It isn't about blaming your parents. It doesn't require forgiveness. The goal of grieving is to find your way home to yourself.

The following chart describes the modified Four Tasks of Grieving. Copy the journal prompts into a notebook.

Grief Task	Journal Prompt
1. Accept the reality that childhood is over—what happened, happened.	Write down all the good things *and* not good things about your childhood. Write down the things you did and *didn't* get to experience. We'll use this list next in the Ritual section.
2. Be willing to feel *all* of your feelings about your childhood (and its finality).	For each item in Task 1, write down your *real* feelings. Don't worry about being mean or hurtful. This exercise is for your eyes only.

Grief Task	Journal Prompt
3. Create new boundaries with friends and family that reflect *your* values.	If you completed your regression list from earlier in the chapter, return to it now. The phrase "If I felt grown and powerful, I would say/do ____ instead." This is the boundary you now get to work on implementing. If setting boundaries changes the relationship, remember— emotional adults can handle other people's disappointment, frustration, and criticism.
4. Take the reins of your life and make decisions based on *your* thoughts, feelings, and dreams.	Focus on the advantages of adulthood. What people, places, and things are available to you now that weren't options when you were a child?

Most people get stuck on Task 1: Accept the reality that childhood is over. What does it mean to accept reality? It means your brain can register the message that childhood is complete. But *how* do you send this message to your brain? One way to move forward is to focus on the advantages of adulthood. You can do this by creating a Do/Be/Have (DBH) list. A DBH list is an inventory of twenty things you want to *do*, twenty things you want to *have*, and twenty things you want to *be*. Another way to approach Task 1 is to create a *ritual*. Cultures from time immemorial have harnessed the power of ritual to mark endings and transitions.

How to Use Rituals in Your Grief Work

We have graduation parties to mark the transition from high school to college. We have birthday parties to celebrate the day we arrived on the planet. Sweet-sixteen parties, weddings, baptisms, and bar mitzvahs are all examples of rituals. But while Western rituals are often emotional and meaningful, they are *not* particularly helpful for marking transitions and honoring endings. Why? When rites of passage become more about the *parents* and the *party* than the *purpose*, it is easy to miss the point and to stay stuck. According to ethnographic research (the study of how people live), rites of passage need to include three phases: separation, liminality, and incorporation.

Separation Phase

This is when you detach from an existing reality—in this case, childhood. You can retain *elements* of your childhood, but there is a separation period where you must leave and recognize what's left behind (the ideals of childhood).

Liminality Phase

This is the uncertain, in-between phase where you have left where you were but you have not quite landed where you're going. If you feel stuck, it's likely that you are in the liminal stage. Grief helps to move you through the liminality phase to the incorporation phase.

Incorporation Phase

Having completed the separation and liminality phases, you can now settle into your new phase of life—emotional adulthood.

Since most modern rituals do *not* include these three phases, you get to make up your own rituals. In *Eat, Pray, Love*, Elizabeth Gilbert writes:

> This is what rituals are for. We do spiritual ceremonies as human beings in order to create a safe resting place for our most complicated feelings of joy or trauma, so we don't have to haul those feelings around with us forever, weighing us down. . . . And I do believe that if your culture or tradition doesn't have the specific ritual you are craving, then you are absolutely permitted to make up a ceremony of your own devising.

Research indicates that self-created ritual is powerful medicine for a wounded heart.*

If you're feeling lost and unsure how to create a ritual, you can use any of the examples that follow. Each ritual includes a sensory element. As you'll recall from chapter 3, sensory elements are key to feeling *safe*, and feeling safe is a prerequisite for getting unstuck. No matter what ritual you choose, remind yourself that the grieving (and healing) process is made up of infinite possibilities. There is no right or wrong way to grieve. If you don't want to do any of these things, don't do them. The more personal and individualized your ritual, the more your brain will be able to lock in the message of Task 1. And remember—these exercises are *not* about grieving the loss of a loved one. They are about grieving the end of the *childhood* you got—or grieving the absence of the childhood you never had.

Rituals for Grieving Childhood

1. *Sensory exercise—earth:* Bury a symbol of your childhood. Say goodbye by writing a eulogy or reading your Task 1 journal list. You can read your list solo or in the presence of a compassionate witness.

2. *Sensory exercise—water:* Take a salt bath or visit a river, lake, or ocean. Imagine saying goodbye to your childhood as you watch

---

* In an interview with Kim Mills for the American Psychological Association, Dr. Michael Norton, the Harold M. Brierley professor of business administration at Harvard Business School, says, "What we find in our research, and this is the good news, is that even those private [rituals] that we make up ourselves, those are associated with less grief and better coping." https://www.apa.org/research/action/speaking-of-psychology/ritual-loss-covid-19. "Recent research suggests that rituals may be more rational than they appear. Why? Because even simple rituals can be extremely effective. . . . What's more, rituals appear to benefit even people who claim not to believe that rituals work. . . . Recently, a series of investigations by psychologists have revealed intriguing new results demonstrating that rituals can have a causal impact on people's thoughts, feelings, and behaviors." Francesca Gino and Michael I. Norton, "Why Rituals Work," *Scientific American*, May 14, 2013. https://www.scientificamerican.com/article/why-rituals-work/.

the water. Imagine your losses disappearing into the waves/
down the drain/etc.

3. *Sensory exercise—fire:* Light a candle in honor of your childhood
   years. You can read your Task 1 list out loud or in your head. As
   you blow out the candle, imagine saying goodbye.

4. *Sensory exercise—air:** Grab a bottle of bubbles. As you breathe
   the bubbles into existence, imagine that they represent your
   childhood. As they pop and disappear, imagine saying goodbye
   to childhood.

5. *Sensory exercise—touch:* Create a memorial to your childhood by
   placing one or more significant objects in a spot where you often
   pass. This can be on the corner of a window, on a shelf, or even
   in the glove compartment of your car.

Some people initially balk at the suggestion to use elements of earth, air,
fire, and water. ("This is *way* too woo-woo for me!") These people are often
surprised to learn there is a *scientific basis* for sensory exercises. Sensory inputs help to bring your thinking brain back online and return you to your
right size. Emotional regression is halted in its tracks when you can "keep
your mind where your feet are."† But remember—rituals are not a one and
done. In other words, the grieving process is not finished after you perform
a ritual. Rituals are intended to help our brains come to terms with the reality of the loss and to keep us moving forward. Loss is painful, but so is staying stuck. The pain of change is usually preferable to the pain of staying the
same. Bestselling author and psychotherapist Lori Gottlieb wrote: "We
can't have change without loss, which is why so often people say they want
change but nonetheless stay exactly the same."

---

* Many people use balloon or lantern releases in grief rituals, but this presents a serious environmental hazard.

† "Keep your mind where your feet are" is a mantra commonly used in the addiction recovery
world.

Conclusion

The most important thing to remember is that childhood is *over*. You made it. *All* of it. You survived birth, infancy, toddlerhood, childhood, and adolescence—for this alone you deserve a *parade*. It is *not* easy to alchemically transform into a functional adult. But just as Alice found her way through the maze of kings and queens, rabbits and madness—so can you. When you successfully transition from emotional childhood to emotional adulthood, small things no longer feel big and big things feel more manageable. Your all-powerful *parents* become regular-sized *people*. At the end of *Alice's Adventures in Wonderland*, our heroine is able to face her fears, leave Wonderland, and return home. In one of the final scenes, Alice is put on trial and surrounded on every side by hostile adversaries. When all seems hopeless, she finds her voice and boldly addresses the villainous Queen of Hearts: "'Who cares for you?' said Alice (she had grown to her full size by this time). 'You're nothing but a pack of cards!'"

BOTTOM-LINE TAKEAWAYS

1. Emotional regression is when you feel smaller and younger than your chronological age and physical size.
2. Signs of emotional regression include indecisiveness, people-pleasing, emotional outbursts, and impostor syndrome.
3. The holiday season is prime time for emotional regression.
4. Asking yourself, *How old do I feel right now?*, can help stop regression.
5. Emotional adults still get to play and be creative and childlike.
6. The solution to emotional regression is grief.
7. Grieving the past frees you from the compulsion to repeat it.
8. Grief does not happen in stages.
9. Most of the things we were taught about grief in Western culture are wrong.

10. There are four tasks to grieving childhood—accept the reality that childhood is over, be willing to feel all your feelings, create new boundaries with friends/family, and take the reins of your life/make decisions based on *your* thoughts/feelings/dreams.

DOS AND DON'TS

Do	Don't
Give yourself time to work through the grieving process. Time does not heal wounds—doing the work of healing is what heals wounds. Take all the time you need.	Think that grief is something you do and then it's done. Grief is like the ocean—some days are sunny and the waters are calm. Other days you tumble and end up with sand in your swimsuit and a mouthful of seaweed.
Use rituals to help your brain process the end of your childhood.	Think you need to do things a specific way. Do whatever rituals make sense for *you*. There's no right way to grieve.
Keep in mind that change can't happen without loss.	Criticize yourself for fearing the pain that comes with change. Change is painful because of the loss involved.
Think about what people, places, and things help you feel adult. Remind yourself of these things during triggering times—especially during the holidays.	Go into the holiday season without a regression plan.

FIVE-MINUTE CHALLENGES

JOURNAL PROMPTS

1. The thing I will miss *most* about being a child is _____
   _____.

2. The thing I will *not* miss about being a child is _____
_____.

3. I'm afraid if I accept childhood is over, that will mean _____
_____.

4. One of the things I'm looking forward to as an emotional adult is
_____
_____.

5. If I felt more adult/emotionally "bigger," I would let myself _____
_____.

CHAPTER 10

Let's Play

Life is like a game of chess.
To win you have to make a move.

—Allan Rufus, *The Master's Sacred Knowledge*

When Netflix aired *The Queen's Gambit* in fall 2020, it ranked number one in sixty-three countries. Based on the novel by Walter Tevis, *The Queen's Gambit* follows prodigy Beth Harmon from tranquilizer-zonked orphan to triumphant chess champion. A seven-hour miniseries about an embattled chess genius seemed unlikely to provoke mass binge-watching. And yet millions of people devoured the show. Beth's razor-sharp brain, sumptuous clothing, and piercing gaze fueled the appeal of the series, but the game of chess was a surprisingly compelling costar. A *New York Times* article said, "in the weeks since *The Queen's Gambit* premiered . . . [chess] sales have grown 125 percent."

There's something alluring about chess. Maybe it's the long history of the game—it's been around for more than 1,500 years. Maybe it's the mystery of the game—chess is simultaneously simple to learn *and* confusing to play. Maybe it's the romance and epic stories associated with castles, knights, kings, and queens. Or maybe we continue to gravitate toward those sixty-four squares because chess is a perfect metaphor for life. Both chess and life are complex and suspenseful. They both require sacrifices. You can play without a strategy, but that doesn't tend to end well. In chess and in life, even a simple pawn can become a powerful queen with enough time and persistence. And sometimes we *all* end up in the unfortunate situation known in chess as zugzwang* —when *any* move you make will end up making a bad situation worse. Thought leaders, scientists, and writers throughout history have compared life to a game of chess. Benjamin Franklin once observed, "The game of chess is not merely an idle amusement. Several very valuable qualities of the mind, useful in the course of human life, are to be acquired or strengthened by it . . . for Life is a kind of Chess, in which we have often points to gain, and competitors or adversaries to contend with."

If you're starting to think, *Umm, that's great, but I'm not a chess person*, you won't need to learn chess to benefit from the tools here. This chapter provides you with an actionable plan for implementing all the concepts and information from this book so you can get unstuck once and for all. Step-by-step programs can quickly lead to inertia, because if one step proves sticky, often the entire effort gets scrapped (as anyone who has ever attempted to put Ikea furniture together knows all too well). Using chess as a metaphor (no knowledge of the actual game required), you'll learn seven simple rules to get yourself out of stuck. You don't need to follow these rules sequentially—feel free to skip around and do whatever makes sense for you on any given day.

---

* "Zugzwang is a German word which basically means, 'It is your turn to move, and all of your moves are bad!' There is no 'pass' or 'skip a move' in chess, so sometimes having to move can lose the game!" https://www.chess.com/article/view/what-is-zugzwang-chess-terms.

The Square of Stuck—Seven Rules

▸ **Rule 1.** Take Inventory
▸ **Rule 2.** Look for Easy Moves
▸ **Rule 3.** Make a List of Three Choices
▸ **Rule 4.** Know Which Pieces You Can and Cannot Move
▸ **Rule 5.** Do One Thing
▸ **Rule 6.** Listen to Feedback
▸ **Rule 7.** Celebrate

Rule 1. Take Inventory

A chessboard has pawns, knights, bishops, rooks, queens, and kings. For our purposes we'll make things *super* easy so you won't need to remember a mess of instructions. Each "piece" on your chessboard represents a single area of life:

- Career
- Money
- Social Life
- Intimate Partner
- Family
- Children/Parenting
- Spirituality
- Creativity
- Physical Health
- Body Image
- Hobbies
- Self-Care
- Mental Health
- Sex
- Purpose
- Community

Identify which pieces make sense for *you* and include whatever categories you want to add. It's easy to get focused on one thing when you're feeling stuck. Taking inventory helps you to see the whole board.

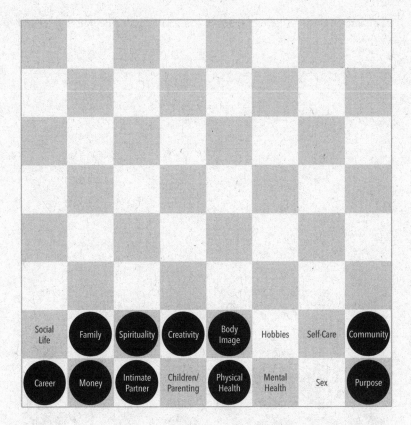

Rule 2. Look for Easy Moves

When you're overwhelmed and under-resourced, it is neither necessary nor helpful to force things. Look for easy moves instead, and do those first. There isn't a specific order you should follow to get unstuck. You may feel trapped at work but find ease with your relationships. You may feel stuck with money but can easily find space for creativity. As long as you do *something*, you're still in the game. *All* moves count—even the easy ones. Once you build momentum from the easy moves, you'll generate enough "I can do this" energy to deal with more difficult areas. And remember that *any* change—even positive change—is going to involve a degree of grief and loss.*

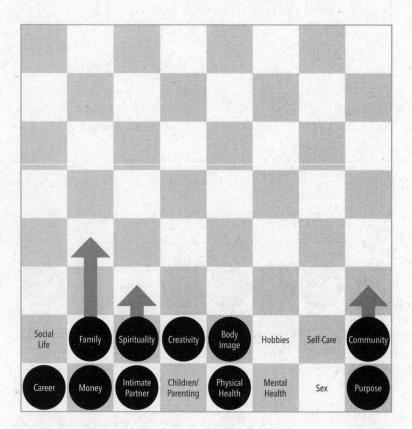

Rule 3. Make a List of Three Choices

Look at your board and see which pieces feel stuck. Write down three *small* choices. For example, if your money piece feels trapped, your three choices may be:

---

* See chapter 9 for how to approach the grieving process.

1. Make a list of all bills that are overdue.
2. Write down the phone numbers of customer service for each of the overdue bills.
3. Call *one* of the bill collectors and set up a payment plan.

If your spirituality piece feels stuck, your three choices may be:

1. Listen to a podcast about spirituality.
2. Ask a friend whom you admire what they do for spiritual practice.
3. Attend a spiritual service. (Even if the service isn't your thing, you'll be able to get a sense of what you do and don't like and then your next choice will be a better fit.)

If your body image piece feels stuck, your three choices may be:

1. Instead of body positivity, go for body *neutrality*. Think of at least *one* part of your body toward which you feel neutral. Thank this part for doing its job.
2. Stop looking in mirrors for a week. (This is a good choice if you yell at yourself every time you see your reflection.)
3. Put all your clothes that don't fit in a box. Put the box in the basement or attic. Nothing creates a shame spiral faster than a daily confrontation with too-tight jeans.

Rule 4. Know Which Pieces You Can and Cannot Move

Most Twelve-Step recovery meetings open with "The Serenity Prayer":*

---

*Original authorship of "The Serenity Prayer" is unknown. Authorship is often attributed to Reinhold Niebuhr, but a 2008 *New York Times* article challenged that assumption. Laurie Goodstein, "Serenity Prayer Stirs Up Doubt: Who Wrote It?" *New York Times,* July 11, 2008. https://www.nytimes.com/2008/07/11/us/11prayer.html.

God, grant me the serenity to accept the things I cannot change
The courage to change the things I can
And the wisdom to know the difference.

You don't need to be in recovery (or to believe in a deity) to benefit from "The Serenity Prayer." It's critical to know the difference between what you *want* to change (but can't) and what you think you *can't* change (but can).

Some of the pieces are in your game because you chose them. And occasionally life puts pieces into play such as postpartum depression or systemic racism that you definitely did *not* choose. Sometimes you can change your circumstances—but not always. Your "board" is a combination of circumstance and choice. And remember, you can't play someone *else's* game. As much as you may *want* your spouse to cut back on their drinking, you can't force them to change. As much as you may *want* your teen to have healthy relationships, you *can't* pick their friends. Your decisions can exert *influence* over your loved ones, but influence is not the same thing as control. The only pieces you can control are your own.

> The only pieces you can control are your own.

Rule 5. Do One Thing

Newton's first law of motion says an object at rest will stay at rest and an object in motion will *stay* in motion unless it's acted upon by an outside force. The same physics applies to your state of stuck. Once you get moving, progress compounds rapidly. Choose *one* task from your list of three and commit to doing it within the next week. Every night before you go to bed write your *one* to-do item on a Post-it or a piece of paper. Then look at it first thing when you wake up.

But wait a minute . . . How am I ever going to get where I want to go if I do only one thing?

A single step forward is preferable to none. Martha Beck calls these mi-

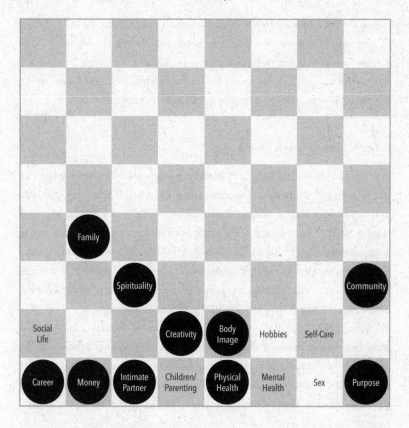

nuscule moves "turtle steps." She says, "A 'turtle step' is the least I can do, divided in half. It's also the only way I've ever achieved anything." When even *small* steps feel impossible, Beck says to break them down to their tiniest components. I remember a phone call with my Twelve-Step sponsor after a particularly horrific meth binge. I hadn't eaten, slept, or showered for days. For close to an hour she talked me through eating a single yogurt spoonful by spoonful. All the clichés that encourage you to take baby steps, to focus on one day at a time, and to do the next right thing* may be overused—but

---

* "Do the next right thing" is one of the mantras of Alcoholics Anonymous. "The Next Right

they exist for a reason. In the dystopian young adult novel *Pawn* by Aimée Carter, one character describes the potential of even the smallest chess pieces. "Because [your pawns] kept moving forward . . . they become the most powerful piece in the game. Never forget that, all right? Never forget the potential one solitary pawn has to change the entire game."

Rule 6. Listen to Feedback

Stuck turns into unstuck the *very second* you take a step—even if you feel like you're going in the wrong direction. Think of the GPS in your car—you will *not* receive instructions if you're parked. GPS kicks in only *after* you start to drive. The beauty of GPS is that even if you start heading the wrong way, you immediately receive feedback. Roadblock? GPS will reroute. Traffic? GPS can maneuver you through side roads. Missed your turn? No problem. Making a wrong turn no longer creates the sweaty palms and panic that it did in the days of MapQuest printouts and gas station directions.[*]

Sometimes it's only *after* we make a wrong move (and learn from it) that the correct move becomes clear. When you take action—*any* action—it's important to pay attention to the feedback and make adjustments as needed. Stuck is often the result of *ignoring* feedback—particularly in early adulthood. Comedian Taylor Tomlinson jokes, "I'm so sick of my twenties. You have no intuition, no instincts . . . there's no mystic, bad feeling under your ribs going 'Hey, maybe *don't* date a DJ . . . *again*.'"[†] Learning from your decisions is as important as the decisions themselves.

Thing" is also a song popularized by Kristen Bell in the movie *Frozen 2*. The earliest known origin of the phrase is from an 1897 book called *Ye Nexte Thynge* by Eleanor Amerman Sutphen. In the book she quotes a poem by Mrs. George A. Paull that includes the lines: "And through the hours / The quiet words ring / Like a low inspiration: / 'Doe ye nexte thynge.'"

[*] If you've ever sat on the side of a road in hysterics because it was pre-GPS and you had no idea which road to take, I see you.

[†] Oh, how I wish Taylor Tomlinson's Netflix special *Quarter-Life Crisis* had been around during my own quarter-life crisis. Brilliant.

Rule 7. Celebrate

There are times when you aren't *actually* stuck but it *seems* like you're stuck because you don't allow yourself to celebrate—or even *validate*—your smaller wins. This might sound like:

- ▸ "Well, yeah, I cooked for myself this week instead of stopping for fast food. But I still have so much weight to lose."
- ▸ "Well, yeah, I made a few payments on my credit card. But I still have so much debt."
- ▸ "Well, yeah, I took a walk this morning. But it's not like I did a 'real' workout."
- ▸ "Well, yeah, I got a bonus. But it's not like I got the promotion I wanted."

I remember the first time my husband saw me celebrate after successfully putting my laundry away the same day I washed it. As a nuclear engineer and former military officer, he was understandably confused by my exuberant joy and celebratory attitude about such a normal aspect of life. But if you've ever struggled with depression, you *know* that a successful transfer of clothing from washing machine to dryer to closet within twenty-four hours is a *major* win. Definitely worth celebrating with DoorDash doughnut delivery.

Saint Francis of Assisi is quoted as saying, "Start by doing what's necessary; then do what's possible; and suddenly you are doing the impossible." It's also important to *celebrate* when you do what's necessary, then *celebrate* again when you do what's possible, and then *really* celebrate when you start doing the impossible.

"But what if everything is going wrong and I have nothing to celebrate?"

I hear you. When things are bleak and dark and sludgy, it's hard to access joy. Celebrating is *not* the same as being positive or grateful during hard times. When things are rough, you *don't* have to play the nauseating game of "good vibes only" or "I'm too blessed to be stressed." You get to be mad and sad and scared and lonely and tired and frustrated and overwhelmed. *And* you get to honor your wins great and small. You get to celebrate your decision to get out of bed—even if you only make it to the couch. You get to celebrate your decision to eat breakfast—especially when you want to restrict. You get to celebrate *any* time you take *any* step. And rest assured—there's neuroscience to back up this crazy notion.[*]

> **Celebrating is a powerful brain hack.**

Celebrating is *not* a frivolous use of your time and energy. Celebrating is a powerful brain hack that can shift your physiology. Celebrations involve music, food, singing, yelling, and dancing/jumping—all of which are *somatic* (body-based). As you saw in chapter 3, body-based interventions reduce stress responses and help you to stay in logical, thinking mode.[†] Celebrating tells your inner security guards, "At ease. We're not being attacked by a tiger. You can stop stimulating our HPA axis now."[‡] If you're unsure how to start celebrating the small stuff, here are some options:

▸ Give yourself permission to eat your favorite dessert.
▸ Give yourself permission *not* to do a chore you think you should do today.

---

[*] Author, CEO, and organizational anthropologist Judith E. Glaser wrote: "Researchers found . . . during celebration time you trigger the basal ganglia system that releases the neurotransmitter dopamine. This chemical communicates with the brain areas in the prefrontal cortex to allow people to pay attention to critical tasks, ignore distracting information, and update only the most relevant task information in working memory during problem-solving tasks." "Celebration Time," *Psychology Today*, December 28, 2015. https://www.psychologytoday.com/us/blog/conversational-intelligence/201512/celebration-time.

[†] See chapter 3 for more information about stress responses. These ideas are intended to be simplifications and metaphors.

[‡] The HPA axis is the hypothalamic-pituitary-adrenal axis. "While proper functioning of the HPA axis is essential for dealing with stress, when the HPA axis is stimulated too much (for example in someone who faces extreme stress on a daily basis), it can lead to physical and psychiatric problems." https://www.neuroscientificallychallenged.com/blog/2014/5/31/what-is-the-hpa-axis.

▸ Purchase or collect something that catches your eye (no need to break the bank—your object can cost a dollar at a vintage store or be an interesting leaf on the side of the road), wrap it in beautiful paper, and write yourself a card that says something like "I'm really proud of you for not giving up today."

▸ Dust off your good plates and good glasses and use them *today*. And tomorrow. And the next day . . .

▸ Light that good candle that you've been saving.

▸ Put out holiday decorations and enjoy them—even if it's the middle of May.

▸ Whatever you do for special occasions, do it *today*.

As hokey, touchy-feely, and Stuart Smalley* as all this sounds, consider the alternative—how effective is your shameful self-talk? Is berating yourself bringing you toward or away from your goals? Pema Chödrön says, "Rejoicing in ordinary things is not sentimental or trite. It actually takes guts. Each time we drop our complaints and allow everyday good fortune to inspire us, we enter the warrior's world."† Legendary science-fiction author Ray Bradbury wrote: "Every time you take a step, even when you don't want to . . . When it hurts, when it means you rub chins with death, or even if it means dying, that's good. Anything that moves ahead, wins. No chess game was ever won by the player who sat for a lifetime thinking over his next move."

---

*Stuart Smalley is a fictional character from *Saturday Night Live* known for his over-the-top self-affirmations: "I'm good enough, I'm smart enough, and doggone it, people like me!"

† Pema Chödrön, *The Places That Scare You: A Guide to Fearlessness in Difficult Times*. In this beautiful book she also writes: "A warrior accepts that we can never know what will happen to us next. We can try to control the uncontrollable by looking for security and predictability, always hoping to be comfortable and safe. But the truth is that we can never avoid uncertainty. This not knowing is part of the adventure, and it's also what makes us afraid."

A Note About Spirituality

Even though this book is about the *science* of stuck, it's impossible to talk about stuck without talking about spirituality. Spirituality is a universal experience—we *all* share the desire for meaning, connection, beauty, and purpose. If you don't cultivate your spirituality, it's almost guaranteed you'll stay stuck. But you *don't* need to believe in a deity to be spiritual. Carl Sagan wrote: "Science is not only compatible with spirituality; it is a profound source of spirituality." There are as many ways to be spiritual as there are to be human. Meditation, mindfulness, cooking, nature, art, mathematics, music, religion—the list of spiritual possibilities is endless. Whether you identify as a devout Catholic, a pagan priestess, or a staunch atheist, it's important to consider whether your spiritual beliefs are there by *choice* or by *default*.

Spirituality is not just what you believe. It is also from whom you take your marching orders. In *Sufi Thought and Action*, Idries Shah wrote: "The human being, whether he realizes it or not, is trusting someone or something every moment of the day." We *all* have an internalized spiritual director. Whose voice is in your head? Whose wrath do you fear? If you make your decisions based on what your neighbor will think, then your neighbor is your spiritual director. If you make decisions because you're afraid of what your mother will say, your mother is your spiritual director. As an emotional adult *you* get to choose your spiritual beliefs and practices. *You* get to decide what to sacrifice and what to save. John O'Donohue writes: "We cannot continue to seek outside ourselves for the things we need from within. The blessings for which we hunger are not to be found in other places or people. These gifts can only be given to you by yourself. They are at home at the hearth of your soul."

Final Thoughts

World champion chess player José Raúl Capablanca y Graupera wrote in the 1920s, "A book cannot by itself teach how to play. It can only serve as a guide, and the rest must be learned by experience." Don't wait until you feel ready to take your turn. You don't need readiness—you need only *willingness*. As you shift out of stuck, expect to encounter discomfort. Stay the course. In trauma work we often use the phrase "A different kind of bad is *good*." A different kind of bad means *change*, and sometimes *changing* feels like *breaking*. But you are unbreakable. There is a hidden place inside *all* of us that remains untouched by trauma, unmarked by injury, and impervious to stuck. Alice Miller wrote: "For the human soul is virtually indestructible, and its ability to rise from the ashes remains as long as the body draws breath."

> You are unbreakable.

You *don't* need to spend the next ten years in psychoanalysis to live your best life. And you don't have to spend hours talking about your childhood to get unstuck. Therapists are archaeologists of the psyche. It's our job to dig deep and unearth ancient patterns. It's our joy to examine artifacts and to discover lost stories. But you'll quickly hit a wall if you believe digging deep is necessary for *everything*. It isn't. Symptom accommodation is a perfectly valid alternative. Symptom accommodation might look like taking medicine, avoiding triggers, or using coping skills. Sometimes deep work is impossible because of children, finances, environment, access to resources, safety, or time. You don't have to get to the root cause of anything if you don't want to go there. All you need to remember is this: You may not know the *origin* of a symptom, but that doesn't mean there isn't a *really* good reason for its presence.

All mental health symptoms are creative manifestations of unmet needs—you are *not* lazy, crazy, or unmotivated. And you don't have to jump off a cliff to get unstuck. Take a small step, see how things go, then take another. Don't forget to celebrate along the way. Jungian psychoanalyst and poet Dr. Clarissa Pinkola Estés writes: "I hope you will go out and let stories, that is life, happen to you, and that you will work with these stories . . . water them with your blood and tears and your laughter till they bloom, till you yourself burst into bloom."

This is *your* life. Your chessboard.

Let's play.

ACKNOWLEDGMENTS

After a descent into madness and the utter annihilation of the life and identity I once knew, I washed up on the shores of a new world. Thank you to the Universe for guides, insights, grace for the journey—and for loving me fiercely. I'm supremely grateful to the scientists, physicians, and researchers for the discoveries cited in these pages and for the many teachers from whom I learned the art and science of psychotherapy. Special thanks to Richard C. Schwartz for creating the Internal Family Systems model of therapy and to Julia Cameron for writing *The Artist's Way*. Finding their work in 2007 dramatically altered the course of my life.

This book wouldn't exist without the otherworldly talents of all the following people and many others. The words *gratitude* and *appreciation* do not begin to describe how I feel about my agent, Rachel Beck, and the team at Liza Dawson Associates. Rachel plucked my proposal out of obscurity, put meat on its bones, and helped me bring it to life. Thank you. You truly are a superhero for books.

I am forever grateful to Marian Lizzi for believing in this project and to her editorial assistant Rachel Ayotte and the entire team at TarcherPerigee for championing this book from conception to birth. Thank you for making my dream a reality.

To my Queen team, who contributed ideas, thoughts, edits, encouragement, and willingness to read sections of the manuscript—Meredith At-wood, Jenn Berry, Pam Breakey, Julie Brooks, Kelly Funk, Latrese Kabuya, Kelly McDaniel, and Jan Saxton-Boyer—thank you. Mega-gratitude goes to my dear friend and fellow trauma therapist Crystle Lampitt—thank you for reading every single word of my early drafts and providing just the right feedback in the moments when I felt frustrated and overwhelmed. Super grateful to my friends and colleagues Nate Postlethwait, Vanessa Cornell, Kristen Asher-Kirk, and Dr. Michelle Robin—thank you for allowing me to use your words. Special thanks to Kathryn McCormick—I'm grateful for your generous contribution on shadows and movement.

Thank you to my soul friend Elise Reid for providing the chess graphics and for eleventh-hour tech saves—*and* for feeding me when I was too broke to buy both food *and* cigarettes in early recovery.

Big thanks to Renaissance woman Sara Page for taking my napkin sketches and producing all of the cartoons and diagrams. Thank you for creating original artwork for my website (and for building the website), for my social media graphics, and for the magical tree mural in my children's therapy office. Thank you for countless hours slugging through business challenges and life crises. Princesses do not grow into queens without high-quality friends, and Sara, you are world-class.

Thank you to the therapists and mentors who scraped me off the ground and showed me a new way to live—Candy Smith, Laura Shaughnessy, and Tracey Bickle; I would not be here without you. Robert Falconer—thank you for never being thrown off by *any* of my inner parts and for lending your wise words to the introduction. Andre de Konig—thank you for being the Jungian wizard who helped me navigate my subconscious. Thank you to Jane Clapp for countless insights into the somatic, psychological, and spiritual—and for being on standby the day I presented to the group of C-suite women mentioned in chapter 6. A big thanks to Jane Friedman for coaching me through the book proposal process. Gratitude to my aerial coach, Elena Sherman—thank you for helping me to get out of my head and into my body, and for reminding me that I don't have to be straight, but my legs do. And thank you to my beloved Sebastian for quietly and patiently accompanying me through the fire until it was your time to cross the Rainbow Bridge.

Thank you to all my clients past, present, and future for trusting me to be a travel guide on their Earth journeys. Deep gratitude to my brilliant friend Dr. Sasha Heinz for writing the foreword and for our friendship—life has been way more fun and work infinitely more inspiring since our paths crossed. Cheers to Medusa and Persephone reimagined.

And finally to my husband, Michael: Thank you for being the most emotionally skilled man I've ever known. Thank you for being my biggest fan and also my biggest critic. Your math-minded engineer perspective challenged me to clarify concepts and to elevate my writing. Thank you for holding space, for loving me exceptionally well, for being the best doggie dad to Oscar, for reminding me how to play, and for cocreating a truly magical life. I love you.

Anderson, Oli. *Shadow Life: Freedom from Bullshit in an Unreal World*. Independently published, 2020.

Barrett, Lisa Feldman. *Seven and a Half Lessons About the Brain*. Mariner, 2020.

Beck, Martha. *Finding Your Own North Star: Claiming the Life You Were Meant to Live*. Three Rivers Press, 2002.

Bernstein, Gabrielle. *The Universe Has Your Back: Transform Fear to Faith*. Hay House Inc., 2016.

Bly, Robert. *A Little Book on the Human Shadow*. HarperOne, 1988.

Bradshaw, John. *Bradshaw On: The Family: A New Way of Creating Solid Self-Esteem*. Health Communications, 1990.

———. *Healing the Shame That Binds You*, expanded and updated ed. Health Communications, 2005.

———. *Homecoming: Reclaiming and Championing Your Inner Child*. Bantam, 1992.

Brown, Brené. *Daring Greatly: How the Courage to Be Vulnerable Transforms the Way We Live, Love, Parent, and Lead*. Avery, 2015.

———. *The Gifts of Imperfection: Let Go of Who You Think You're Supposed to Be and Embrace Who You Are*. Hazelden, 2010.

Cameron, Julia. *The Artist's Way: A Spiritual Path to Higher Creativity, 25th Anniversary Edition*. TarcherPerigee, 2016.

Campbell, Joseph. *The Hero with a Thousand Faces: The Collected Works of Joseph Campbell*. New World Library, 2008.

Chapman, Gary. *The Five Love Languages: The Secret to Love That Lasts*. Northfield, 2015.

——. *Things I Wish I'd Known Before We Got Married*. Northfield, 2010.

Chödrön, Pema. *The Places That Scare You: A Guide to Fearlessness in Difficult Times*. Shambhala, 2002.

Dana, Deb. *The Polyvagal Theory in Therapy: Engaging the Rhythm of Regulation*. W. W. Norton, 2018.

Earley, Jay. *Self-Therapy: A Step-by-Step Guide to Creating Wholeness and Healing Your Inner Child Using IFS, a New Cutting-Edge Therapy*, 2nd ed. Pattern System Books, 2009.

Estés, Clarissa Pinkola. *Women Who Run with the Wolves: Myths and Stories of the Wild Woman Archetype*. Ballantine, 1996.

Fadiman, James, and Jordan Gruber. *Your Symphony of Selves: Discover and Understand More of Who We Are*. Park Street Press, 2020.

Faigel, Harris C. *Alchemy: How Adolescence Changes Children into Adults*. Quill House Publishers, 2012.

Fisher, Janina. *Healing the Fragmented Selves of Trauma Survivors: Overcoming Internal Self-Alienation*. Routledge, 2017.

Forward, Susan, with Donna Frazier Glynn. *Mothers Who Can't Love: A Healing Guide for Daughters*. Harper Paperbacks, 2014.

Frances, Allen. *Saving Normal: An Insider's Revolt Against Out-of-Control Psychiatric Diagnosis, DSM-5, Big Pharma, and the Medicalization of Ordinary Life*. William Morrow Paperbacks, 2014.

Frankl, Viktor E., with a foreword by Harold S. Kushner. *Man's Search for Meaning*. Beacon Press, 2006.

Gilbert, Elizabeth. *Big Magic: Creative Living Beyond Fear*. Penguin, 2016.

Gottlieb, Lori. *Maybe You Should Talk to Someone: A Therapist, Her Therapist, and Our Lives Revealed*. Mariner Books, 2019.

Gottman, John. *The Relationship Cure: A Five-Step Guide to Strengthening Your Marriage, Family, and Friendships*. Harmony, 2002.

Hari, Johann. *Lost Connections: Why You're Depressed and How to Find Hope*. Bloomsbury, 2018.

Hendricks, Gay. *The Big Leap: Conquer Your Hidden Fear and Take Life to the Next Level*. Harper, 2010.

Hendrix, Harville, and Helen LaKelly Hunt. *Getting the Love You Want: A Guide for Couples*, revised, updated ed. St. Martin's Griffin, 2019.

Johnson, Robert A. *Owning Your Own Shadow: Understanding the Dark Side of the Psyche*. HarperSanFrancisco, 1993.

Jung, Carl C. *Modern Man in Search of a Soul,* trans. W. S. Dell and Cary F. Baynes. Harcourt Brace, 1955.

Lee, John. *Growing Yourself Back Up: Understanding Emotional Regression*. Three Rivers Press, 2001.

Levine, Peter A. *Trauma and Memory: Brain and Body in a Search for the Living Past: A Practical Guide for Understanding and Working with Traumatic Memory*. North Atlantic Books, 2015.

Levine, Peter A., with Ann Frederick. *Waking the Tiger: Healing Trauma*. North Atlantic Books, 1997.

Lewis, Marc. *The Biology of Desire: Why Addiction Is Not a Disease*. PublicAffairs, 2016.

Love, Patricia, with Jo Robinson. *The Emotional Incest Syndrome: What to Do When a Parent's Love Rules Your Life*. Bantam, 1991.

Maté, Gabor. *When the Body Says No: Exploring the Stress-Disease Connection*. Wiley, 2011.

Maté, Gabor, and Peter A. Levine. *In the Realm of Hungry Ghosts: Close Encounters with Addiction*. North Atlantic Books, 2010.

McDaniel, Kelly. *Mother Hunger: How Adult Daughters Can Understand and Heal from Lost Nurturance, Protections, and Guidance*. Hay House, 2021.

Mellody, Pia, Andrea Wells Miller, and J. Keith Miller. *Facing Codependence: What It Is, Where It Comes from, How It Sabotages Our Lives*. Harper, 2003.

Mellody, Pia, and Lawrence S. Freundlich. *The Intimacy Factor: The Ground Rules for Overcoming the Obstacles to Truth, Respect, and Lasting Love*. HarperSanFrancisco, 2003.

Miller, Alice. *The Body Never Lies: The Lingering Effects of Hurtful Parenting*, trans. Andrew Jenkins. W. W. Norton, 2006.

——. *The Drama of the Gifted Child: The Search for the True Self*, revised, updated ed., trans. Ruth Ward. Basic Books, 2007.

——. *For Your Own Good: Hidden Cruelty in Child-Rearing and the Roots of Violence*, 3rd ed. Farrar, Straus and Giroux, 1990.

O'Donohue, John. *Anam Cara: A Book of Celtic Wisdom*. Harper Perennial, 1998.

Ogden, Pat, Kekuni Minton, and Clare Pain. *Trauma and the Body: A Sensorimotor Approach to Psychotherapy*. W. W. Norton, 2006.

Pearson, Carol S. *Persephone Rising: Awakening the Heroine Within*. HarperOne, 2015.

Peck, M. Scott. *The Road Less Traveled, Timeless Edition: A New Psychology of Love, Traditional Values, and Spiritual Growth*. Touchstone, 2003.

Perel, Esther. *Mating in Captivity: Unlocking Erotic Intelligence*. Harper Paperbacks, 2017.

Pinker, Susan. *The Village Effect: How Face-to-Face Contact Can Make Us Healthier and Happier*. Random House Canada, 2014.

Porges, Stephen W. *The Pocket Guide to the Polyvagal Theory: The Transformative Power of Feeling Safe*. W. W. Norton, 2017.

Pressfield, Steven. *The War of Art: Break Through the Blocks and Win Your Inner Creative Battles*. Black Irish Entertainment, 2002.

Resch, Elyse, and Evelyn Tribole. *Intuitive Eating: A Revolutionary Program That Works*, 3rd ed. St. Martin's Griffin, 2012.

Rosenberg, Marshall B. *Nonviolent Communication: A Language of Life*, 3rd ed. PuddleDancer Press, 2015.

Roth, Geneen. *This Messy Magnificent Life: A Field Guide to Mind, Body, and Soul*. Scribner, 2019.

Schwartz, Richard C., and Robert R. Falconer. *Many Minds, One Self: Evidence for a Radical Shift in Paradigm*. Center for Self Leadership, 2017.

Schwartz, Richard C., and Martha Sweezy. *Internal Family Systems Therapy*, 2nd ed. Guilford Press, 2020.

Siegel, Daniel J. *The Developing Mind: How Relationships and the Brain Interact to Shape Who We Are*, 3rd ed. Guilford, 2020.

Singh, Awdesh. *31 Ways to Happiness*. Balaji World of Books.

Szasz, Thomas S. *The Myth of Mental Illness: Foundations of a Theory of Personal Conduct*. Harper Perennial, 2010.

Tatkin, Stan. *Wired for Love: How Understanding Your Partner's Brain and Attachment Style Can Help You Defuse Conflict and Build a Secure Relationship*. New Harbinger Publications, 2012.

Tawwab, Nedra Glover. *Set Boundaries, Find Peace*. TarcherPerigee, 2021.

Turner, Toko-pa. *Belonging: Remembering Ourselves Home*. Her Own Room Press, 2017.

van der Kolk, Bessel. *The Body Keeps the Score: Brain, Mind, and Body in the Healing of Trauma*. Penguin, 2015.

van Gennep, Arnold. *The Rites of Passage,* 2nd ed., trans. Monika B. Vizedom and Gabrielle L. Caffee. University of Chicago Press, 2019.

Walker, Pete. *Complex PTSD: From Surviving to Thriving: A Guide and Map for Recovering from Childhood Trauma*. CreateSpace Independent Publishing Platform, 2013.

———. *The Tao of Fully Feeling: Harvesting Forgiveness out of Blame*. CreateSpace Independent Publishing Platform, 2015.

Watters, Ethan. *Crazy Like Us: The Globalization of the American Psyche*. Free Press, 2011.

Whitaker, Robert. *Anatomy of an Epidemic: Magic Bullets, Psychiatric Drugs, and the Astonishing Rise of Mental Illness in America*. Crown, 2011.

Williamson, Marianne. *A Return to Love: Reflections on the Principles of "A Course in Miracles,"* reissue ed. HarperOne, 1996.

Wolynn, Mark. *It Didn't Start with You: How Inherited Family Trauma Shapes Who We Are and How to End the Cycle*. Penguin Life, 2017.

Worden, J. William. *Grief Counseling and Grief Therapy: A Handbook for the Mental Health Practitioner*, 5th ed. Springer, 2018.

Zweig, Connie, and Steve Wolf. *Romancing the Shadow: Illuminating the Dark Side of the Soul*. Ballantine, 1997.

Alexander, Bobby C. "Rite of Passage." *Encyclopaedia Britannica*. https://www.britannica.com/topic/rite-of-passage.

Callahan, Molly. "It's Time to Correct Neuroscience Myths." Northeastern University College of Science, April 18, 2019. https://cos.northeastern.edu/news/its-time-to-correct-neuroscience-myths/.

Mobbs, Dean, Ralph Adolphs, Michael S. Fanselow et al. "On the Nature of Fear." Originally published in *Nature Neuroscience* 22 (2019): 1205–16. Reprinted in *Scientific American*: https://www.scientificamerican.com/article/on-the-nature-of-fear/.

Moser, Jason S., Adrienne Dougherty, Whitney I. Mattson et al. "Third-Person Self-Talk Facilitates Emotion Regulation Without Engaging Cognitive Control: Converging Evidence from ERP and fMRI." *Scientific Reports* 7, no. 1 (December 2017): article 4519. https://doi.org/10.1038/s41598-017-04047-3.

Pilecki, B. C., J. W. Clegg, and D. McKay. "The Influence of Corporate and Political Interests on Models of Illness in the Evolution of the DSM." *European Psychiatry* 26, no. 3 (2011): 194–200. https://doi.org/10.1016/j.eurpsy.2011.01.005.

Sjöblom, Margareta, Kerstin Öhrling, Maria Prellwitz, and Catrine Kostenius. "Health Throughout the Lifespan: The Phenomenon of the Inner Child Reflected in Events During Childhood Experienced by Older Persons." *International Journal of Qualitative Studies on Health and Well-Being* 11, no. 1 (2016): 31486. https://doi.org/10.3402/qhw.v11.31486.

Sutton, Jon, ed. "Lisa Feldman Barrett: 'Many Fairy Tales About the Brain Still Propagate Through Our Field.'" *The Psychologist* 30 (April 2017): 54–57. https://thepsychologist.bps.org.uk/volume-30/april-2017/many-fairy-tales-about-brain-still-propagate-through-our-field.

"What Causes Depression?" Harvard Health Publishing, June 24, 2019. https://www.health.harvard.edu/mind-and-mood/what-causes-depression.